Flying Origami Stuff

airplanes and more

...for Ali and Ale and for all the boys
and girls from 0 to 100 years old.

train your Brain

Index

Index

tomono ta

Introduction

Welcome all you flight and origami enthusiasts! Dive into the captivating world of flying papers with us. It's a realm that blends the art of origami, where you fold a material as simple as paper, with the science behind aerodynamics and aviation.

Origami 折り紙

Let's remember that Origami is and art form that involves folding paper to create figures, without using glue or scissors. If you want to delve into origami, we recommend our series of books Useful Origami Stuff (available on Amazon). With these, you can practice and gain skill in this fascinating art.

In this book, you'll find many models and different ways to make paper airplanes. While we may not be manufacturing massive planes like the ones in the sky, our paper models are just as thrilling. Besides, both kinds follow the same physical rules, wich we'll tell you about later, and you can experience them in a fun way.

Following the instructions, you'll learn to fold and crease to achieve simple models that can perform spectacular flights. And don't worry, you don't need an aerospace engineering degree to join this adventure! We"ll guide you step by step with our diagrams, and yu'll achieve truly surprising results.

Ready to impress your family and friends?

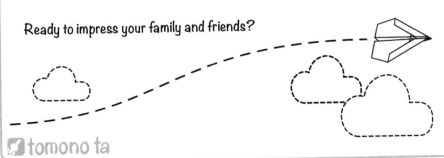

Making paper airplanes isn't just fun; it also offers numerous benefits, both educational and entertaining. Among them, we can highlight:

- Cretivity: sparks creativity and design thinking. Experimenting with different shapes and folding techniques stimulates imagination and artistic skills.

- Practical Physics learning: It's a hand-on opportunity to grasp important physics principles like aerodinamycs, gravity and air resistance.

- Fine Motor Skills Development: Folding, creasing and launching paper airplanes aid in developing fine motor skills in both children and adults. This activity involves precise hand and finger movements, beneficial for hand- eye coordination.

- Stress Reduction and Fun: It's a relaxing and enjoyable activity. Throwing airplanes and watching them soar is a stress relieving and fun way to spend time, whether alone or with company.

- Inclusive Activity: Suitable for anyone, regardless of age or ability. Even better when shared with family or friends.

- Inspiring Activity: Fosters interest in science and technology and may ignite a desire to learn more about aviation or Origami.

In summary, paper airplanes offer significant benefits beyond inmediate fun, from practical skill development to exploring scientific concepts.

Why do airplanes fly?

Although paper airplanes may seem simple, their flight is based on some key physics principles related to aerodynamics. It's important to note that these principles are the same as those applied to large passenger planes:

- Lift (Bernoulli's Principle): the air passing over the plane's wing has to cover a greater distance than the air passing underneath in the same time. This creates a pressure difference, resulting in an upward force known as lift, wich keeps airplanes in the air!

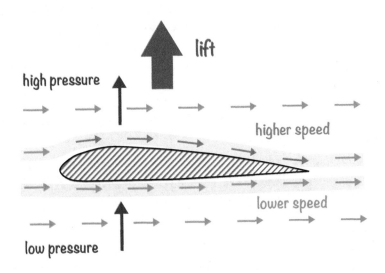

lift

high pressure

higher speed

lower speed

low pressure

- Gravity: While lift helps the airplane stay a loft, there's also a opposing force making the airplane fall: gravity. But if lift is strong enough, the airplane can stay in flight for a while!

- Stability and Center of Gravity: It's crucial to consider the center of gravity. It's the point where the weight of the airplane is concentrated and balanced. A well-balanced airplane, with the center of gravity properly located, will fly farther.

- Air Ressistance: We need some air ressistance to stabilize the airplane. Depending on the shape of the airplane, it will interact with the air better or worse, allowing for more or less controlled flight.

In summary, a paper airplane's flight depends on the lift that raises it and the gravity that pulls it down. By understanding these basic principles, you can adjust and experiment with your airplane to achieve better and longer flights!

As you progress through this book, you'll create different designs and shapes, experimenting to discover why some fly better than others, exploring these basic principles of aeronautics.

Finally, we've included in this book some models that are more artistic than technical. Although these models aren't specifically designed to fly, they are related to the world of air aerodynamics. Executing and observing them will also provide moments of fun and enjoyment.

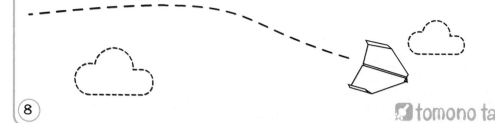

Airplanes

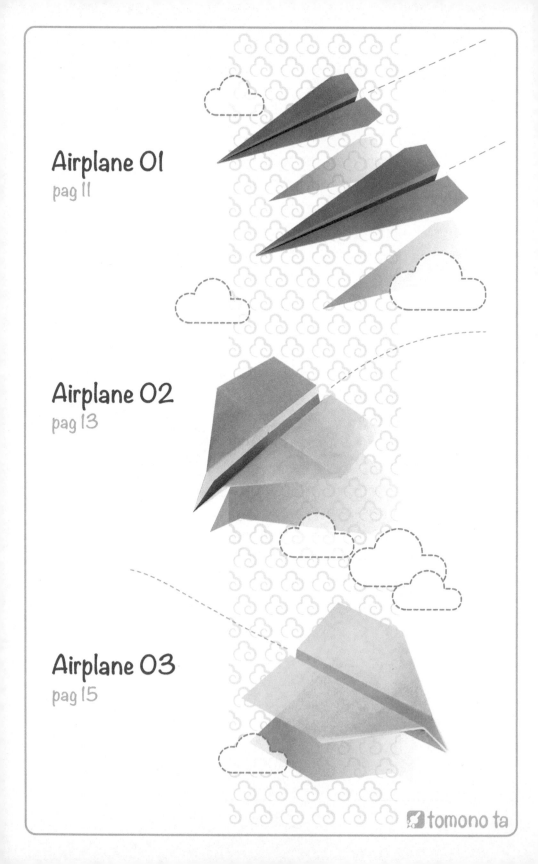

tomono ta

Airplane 01

1 sheet in A4 or letter size format

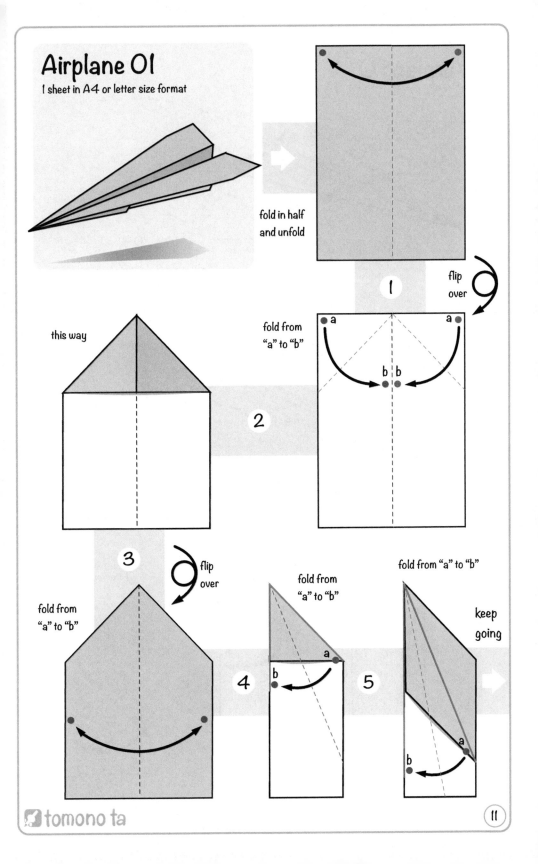

fold in half and unfold

1

flip over

fold from "a" to "b"

a a

b b

2

this way

3

flip over

fold from "a" to "b"

fold from "a" to "b"

a
b

4

fold from "a" to "b"

5

a
b

keep going

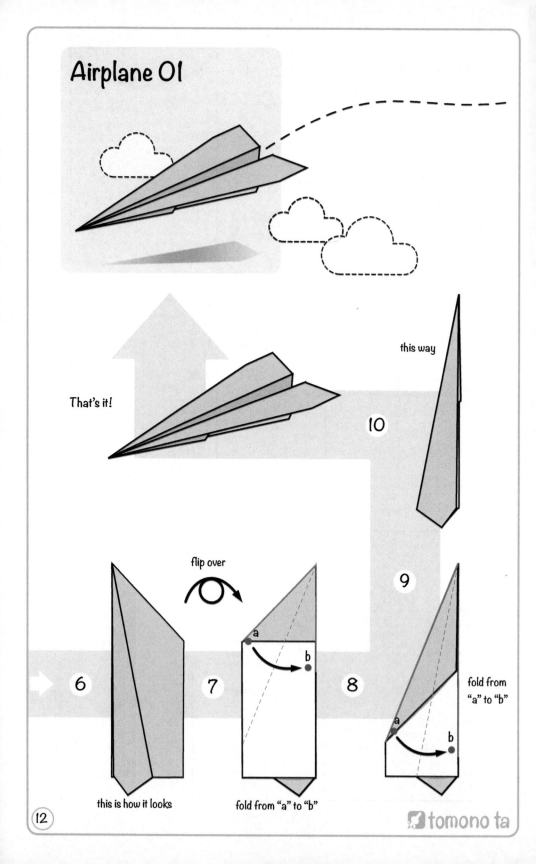

Airplane 01

That's it!

this way

10

9

flip over

6 — this is how it looks

7 — fold from "a" to "b"

a
b

8 — fold from "a" to "b"

a
b

12

tomono ta

Airplane 02

1 sheet in A4 or letter size format

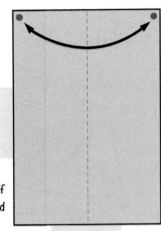

fold in half
and unfold

1

fold from
"a" to "b"

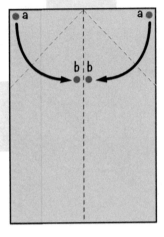

2

fold from
"a" to "b"

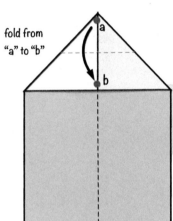

3

fold from
"a" to "b"

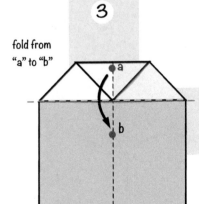

4

fold from "a" to "b"   keep going

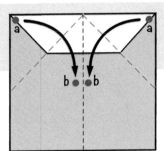

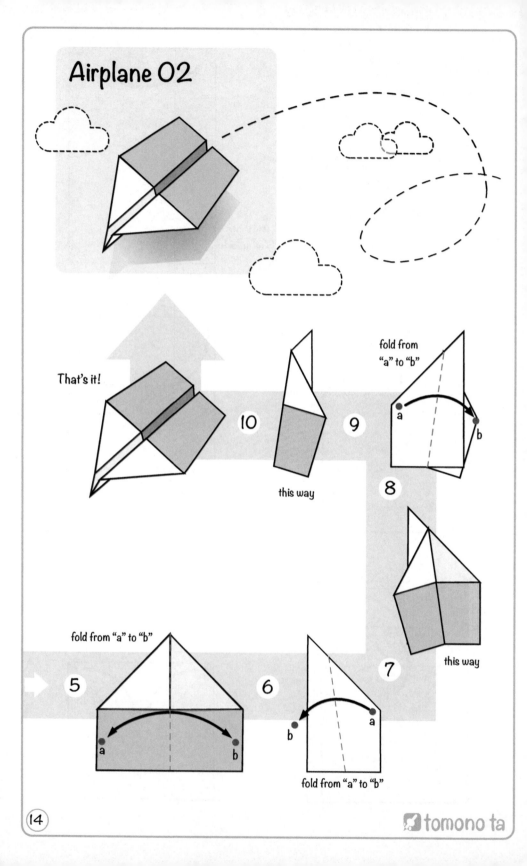

Airplane 02

That's it!

10

9

fold from "a" to "b"

a → b

this way

8

this way

7

fold from "a" to "b"

a ←→ b

5

6

b ← a

fold from "a" to "b"

tomono ta

Airplane 03

I sheet in A4 or letter size format

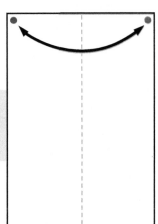

fold in half
and unfold

1

fold from "a" to "b"

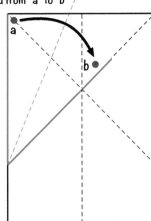

fold from
"a" to "b"
and unfold

2

3

fold from "a" to "b"

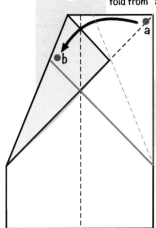

4

fold from
"a" to "b"

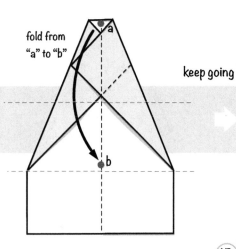

keep going

Airplane 03

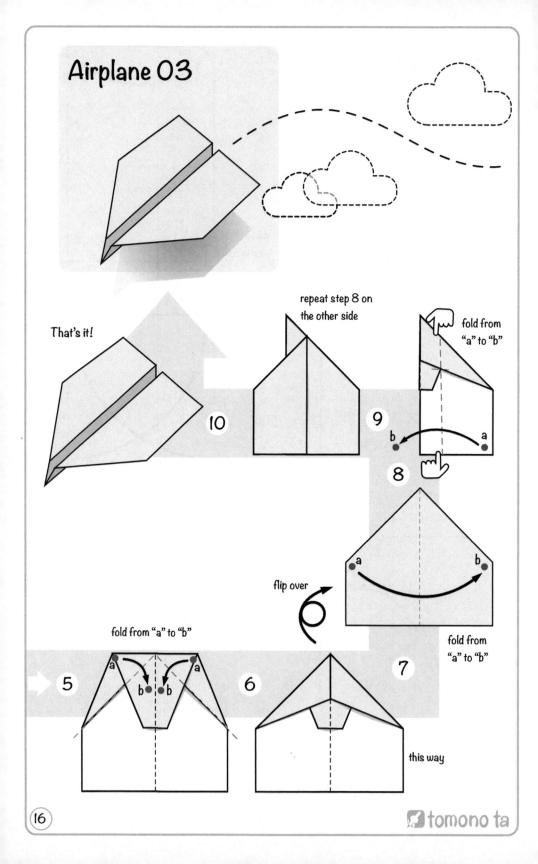

That's it!

repeat step 8 on
the other side

fold from
"a" to "b"

10

9

b ● ● a

8

flip over

a ● ● b

fold from
"a" to "b"

fold from "a" to "b"

5

a ● ● a
b ● ● b

6

7

this way

tomono ta

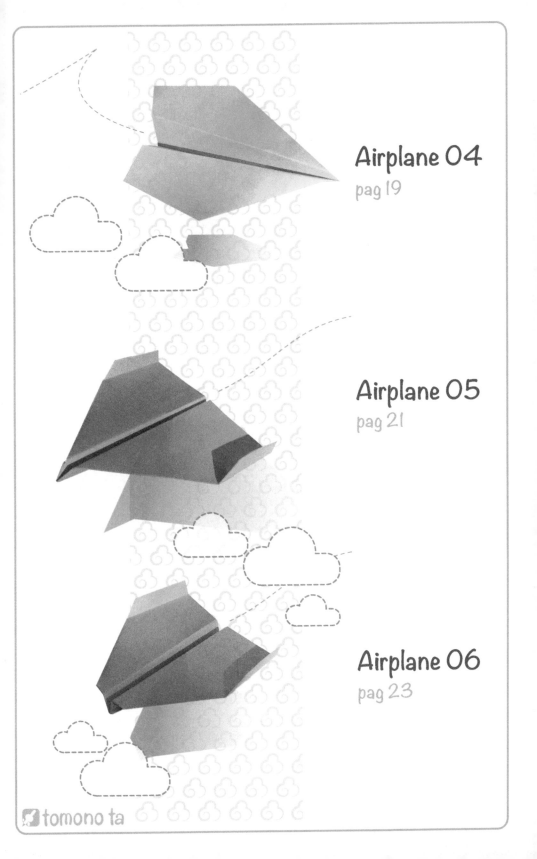

tomono ta

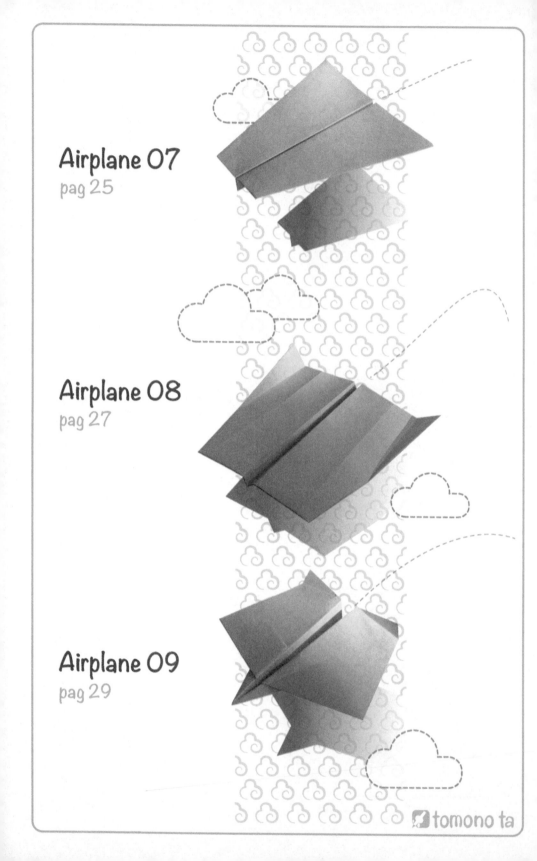

tomono ta

Airplane 04

I sheet in A4 or letter size format

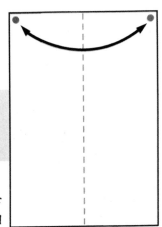

fold in half and unfold

1

fold in half and unfold

2

fold from "a" to "b" and unfold

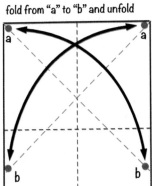

a   a

b   b

3

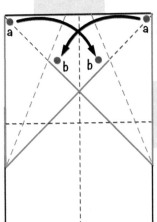

a   a

b b

fold from "a" to "b"

4

fold from "a" to "b"

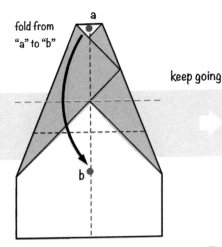

a

b

keep going

Airplane 04

That's it!

repeat step 8 on the other side

fold from "a" to "b"

9

8

fold from "a" to "b"

a • ——————————————— • b

flip over

7

fold from "a" to "b"

a • • a
b • • b

5

6

b •
a •

fold from "a" to "b"

tomono ta

Airplane 05

1 sheet in A4 or letter size format

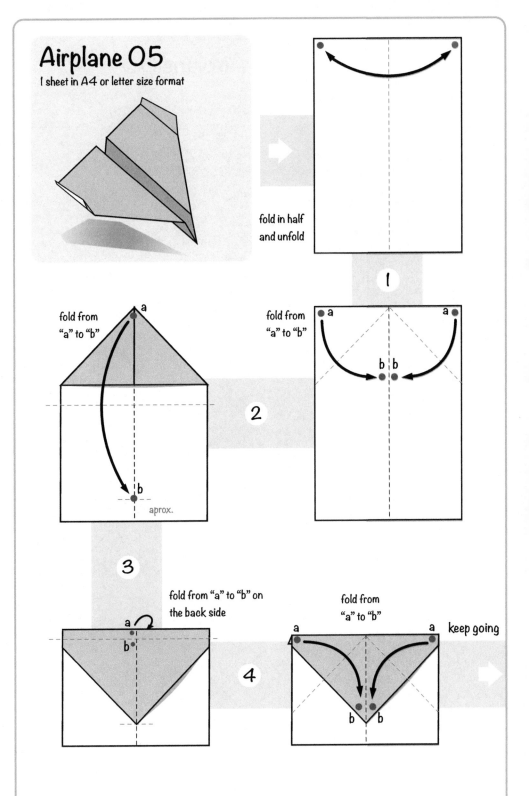

fold in half and unfold

1

fold from "a" to "b"

2

fold from "a" to "b"

aprox.

3

fold from "a" to "b" on the back side

4

fold from "a" to "b"

keep going

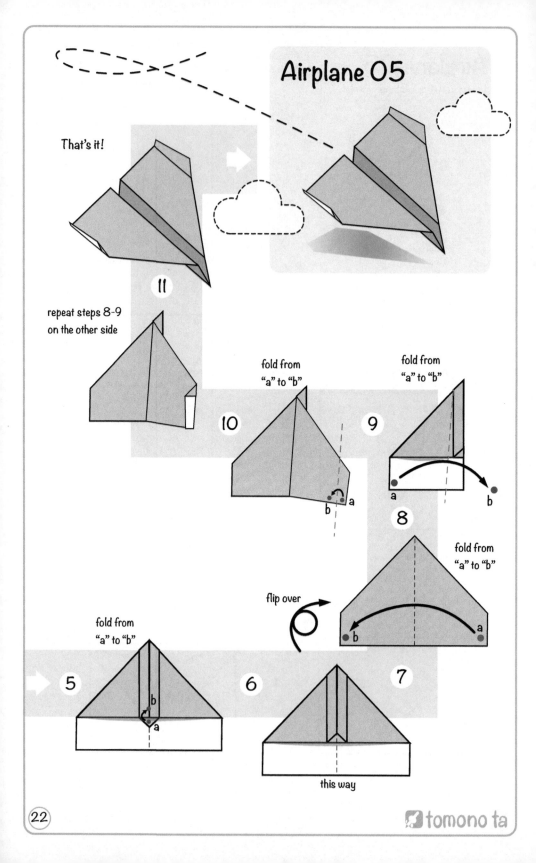

Airplane 05

That's it!

11

repeat steps 8-9
on the other side

10

fold from
"a" to "b"

b a

9

fold from
"a" to "b"

a b

8

fold from
"a" to "b"

b a

flip over

fold from
"a" to "b"

5 b a

6

this way

7

tomono ta

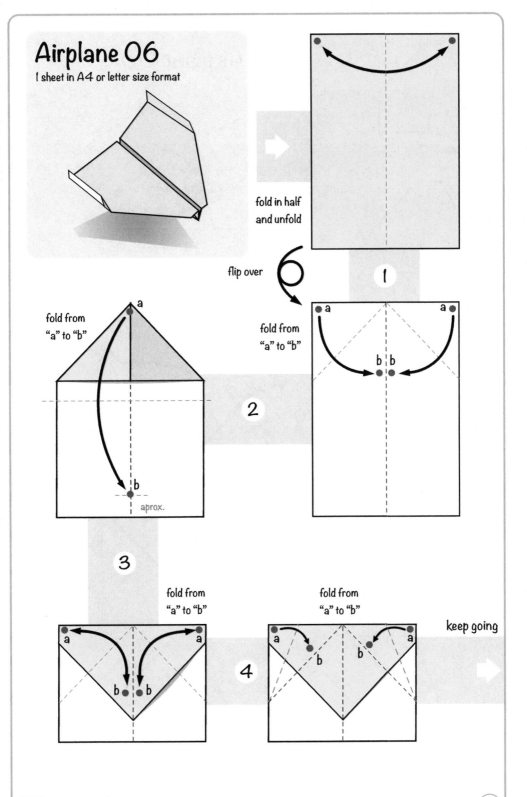

Airplane 06

I sheet in A4 or letter size format

fold in half
and unfold

1

flip over

fold from
"a" to "b"

2

fold from
"a" to "b"

3

aprox.

fold from
"a" to "b"

4

fold from
"a" to "b"

keep going

tomono ta

23

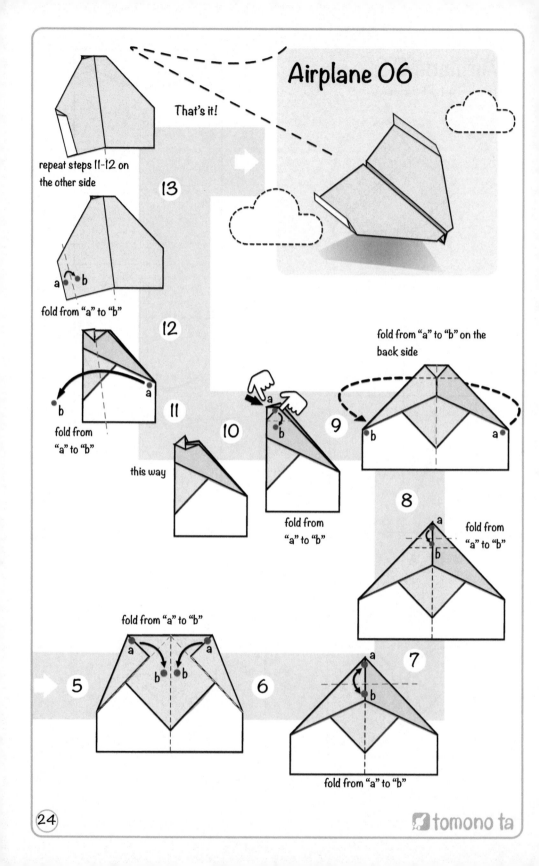

Airplane 06

repeat steps 11-12 on the other side

That's it!

13

fold from "a" to "b"

12

fold from "a" to "b"

11

this way

10

fold from "a" to "b"

9

fold from "a" to "b" on the back side

8

fold from "a" to "b"

5

fold from "a" to "b"

6

7

fold from "a" to "b"

tomono ta

Airplane 07

1 sheet in A4 or letter size format

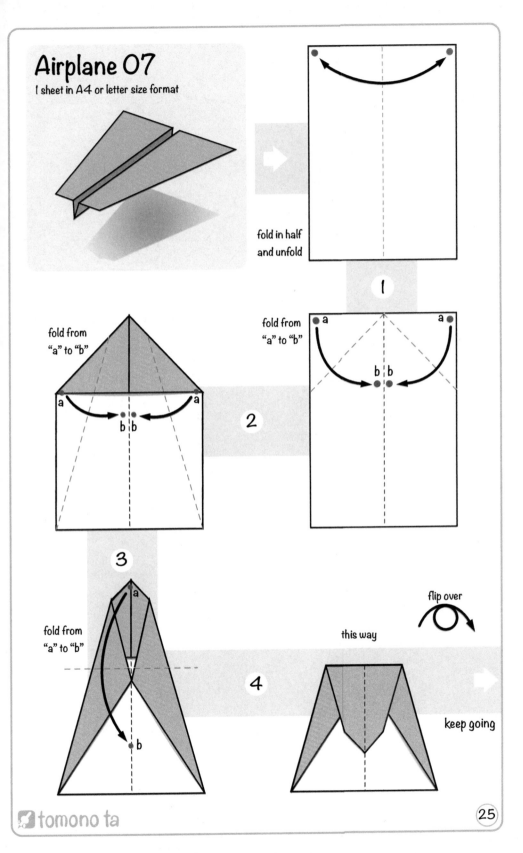

fold in half
and unfold

1

fold from
"a" to "b"

2

fold from
"a" to "b"

3

fold from
"a" to "b"

4

this way

flip over

keep going

Airplane 07

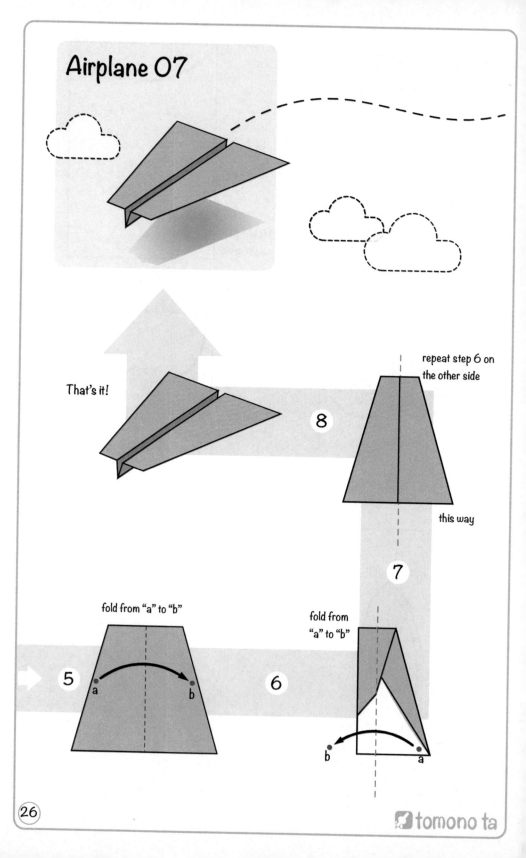

That's it!

8

repeat step 6 on the other side

this way

7

5 fold from "a" to "b"
a   b

6 fold from "a" to "b"
b   a

tomono ta

Airplane 08

1 square sheet of paper

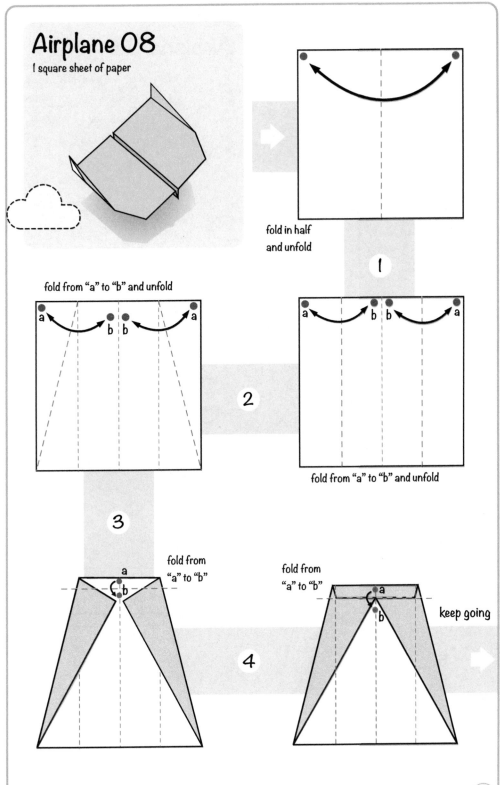

fold in half
and unfold

1

fold from "a" to "b" and unfold

2

fold from "a" to "b" and unfold

3

fold from "a" to "b"

4

fold from "a" to "b"

keep going

tomono ta

(27)

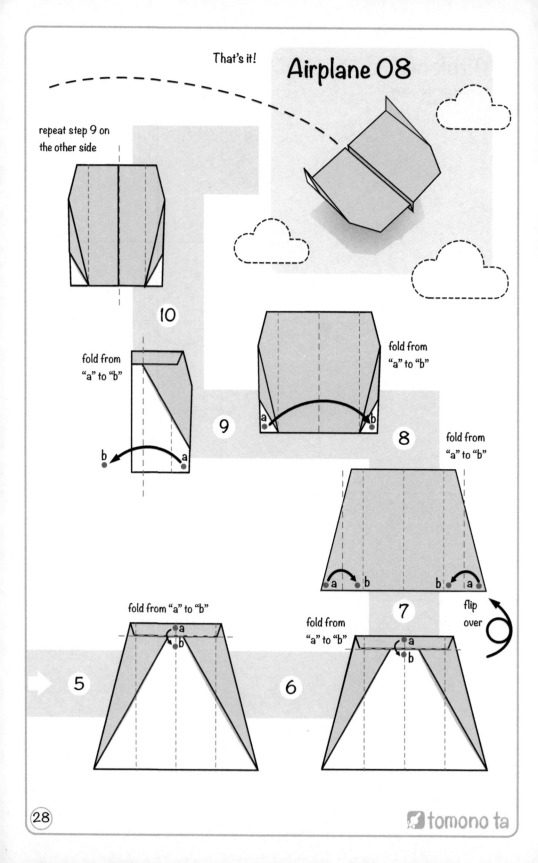

That's it!

Airplane 08

repeat step 9 on the other side

10

fold from "a" to "b"

b   a

9

fold from "a" to "b"

a   b

8

fold from "a" to "b"

a   b   b   a

7

flip over

fold from "a" to "b"

a
b

5

fold from "a" to "b"

a
b

6

tomono ta

Airplane 09

1 sheet in A4 or letter size format

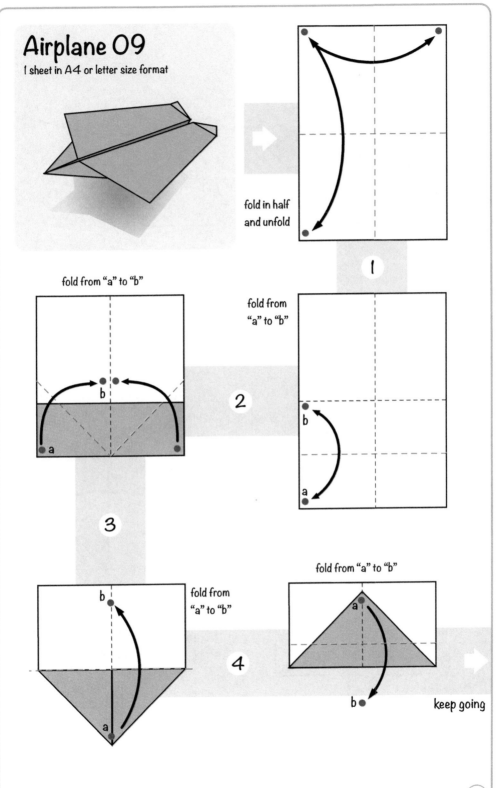

fold in half and unfold

1

fold from "a" to "b"

2

fold from "a" to "b"

3

fold from "a" to "b"

4

fold from "a" to "b"

keep going

Airplane 09

repeat step 7 on the other side

fold from "a" to "b"

That's it!

9

8

fold from "a" to "b"

b

a

7

flip over

this way

5

6

fold from "a" to "b"

a

b

fold from "a" to "b"

tomono ta

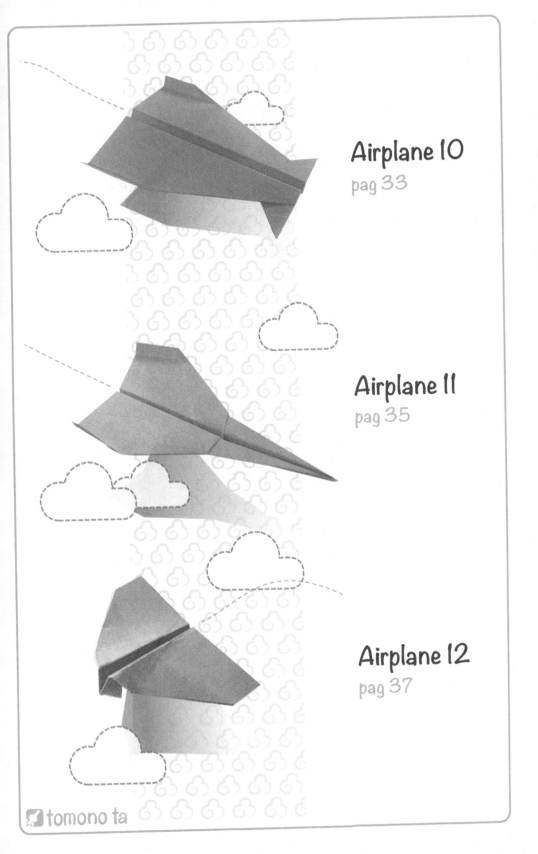

Airplane 10
pag 33

Airplane 11
pag 35

Airplane 12
pag 37

tomono ta

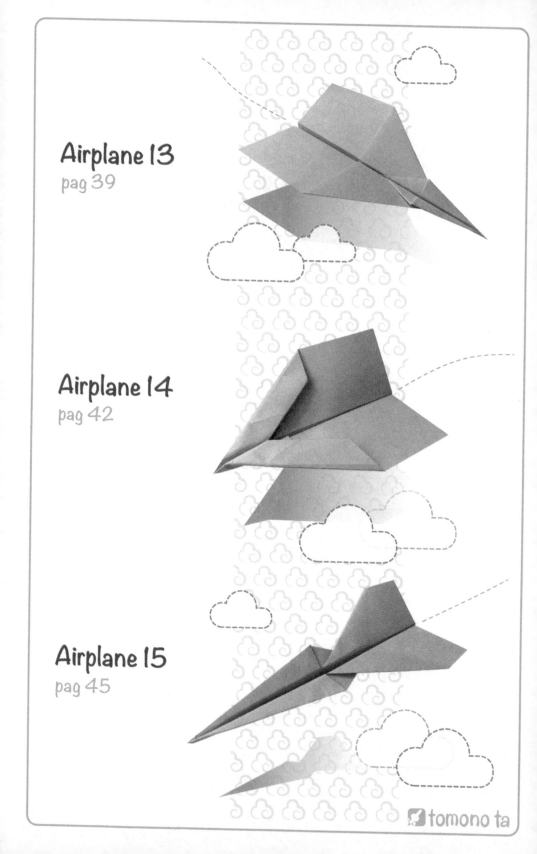

Airplane 13
pag 39

Airplane 14
pag 42

Airplane 15
pag 45

tomono ta

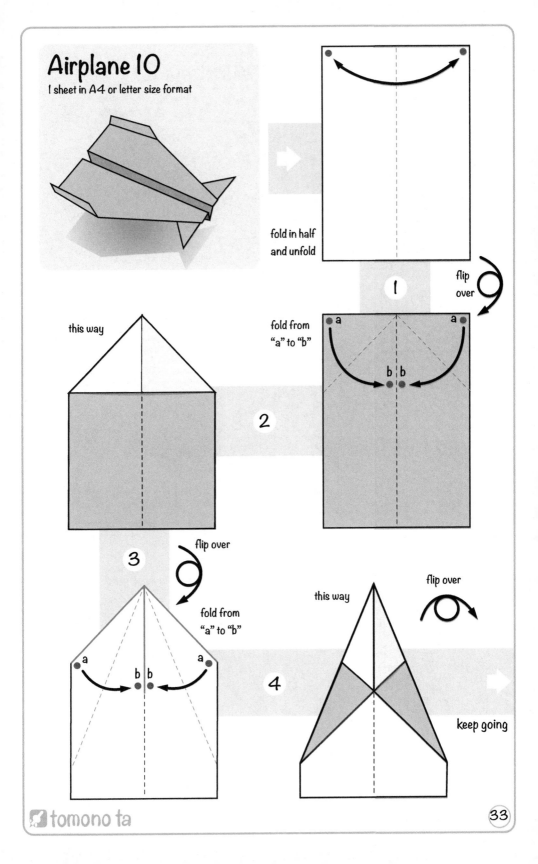

Airplane 10

I sheet in A4 or letter size format

fold in half
and unfold

1

flip over

fold from "a" to "b"

a · · a

b · · b

2

this way

3

flip over

fold from "a" to "b"

a · b · b · a

4

this way

flip over

keep going

tomono ta

33

Airplane 10

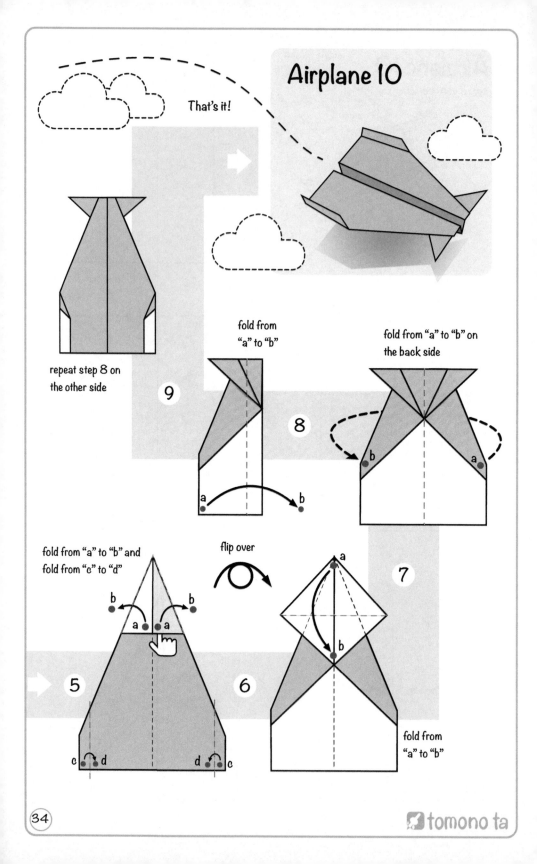

That's it!

repeat step 8 on the other side

fold from "a" to "b"

9

8

fold from "a" to "b" on the back side

b   a

fold from "a" to "b" and fold from "c" to "d"

b   b
a   a

5

c d   d c

flip over

6

a

b

7

fold from "a" to "b"

tomono ta

Airplane II

1 sheet in A4 or letter size format

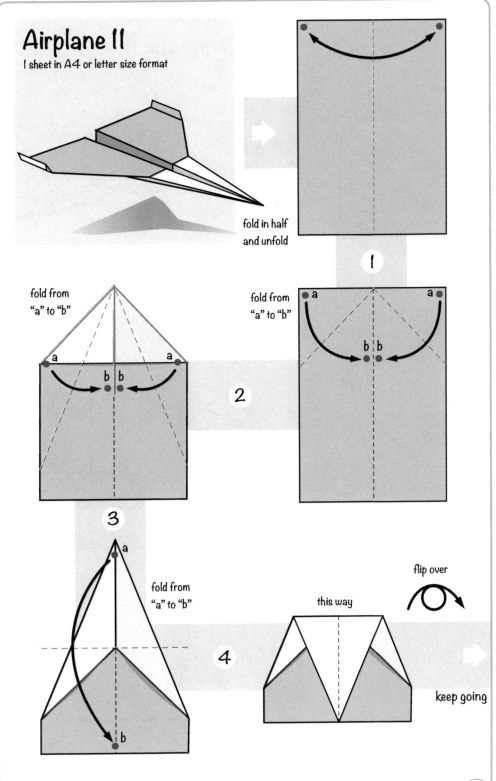

fold in half and unfold

1

fold from "a" to "b"

2

fold from "a" to "b"

3

fold from "a" to "b"

4

this way

flip over

keep going

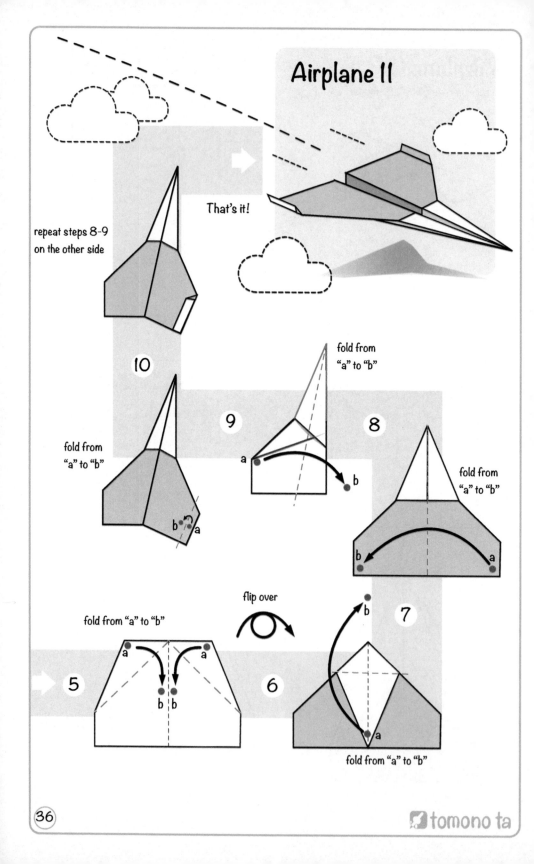

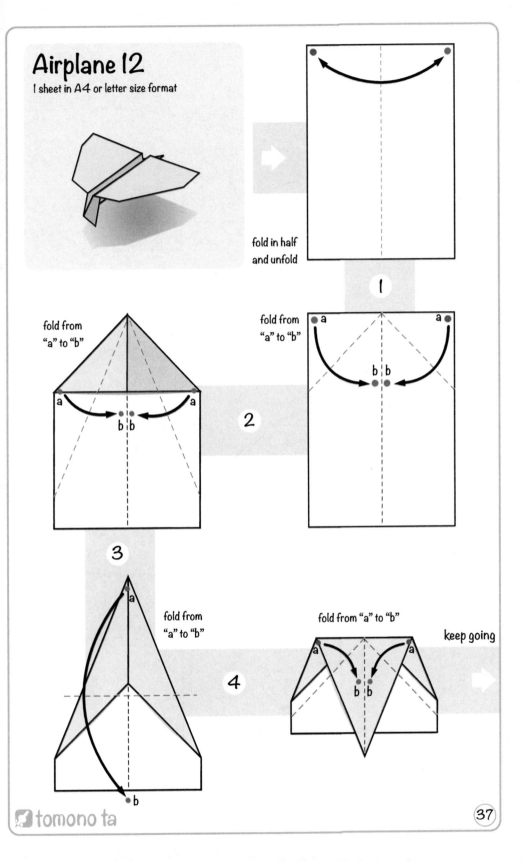

Airplane 12

I sheet in A4 or letter size format

fold in half and unfold

1

fold from "a" to "b"

2

fold from "a" to "b"

3

fold from "a" to "b"

4

fold from "a" to "b"

keep going

Airplane 12

that's it!

10

repeat step 9 on the other side

9

fold from "a" to "b"

fold from "a" to "b" on the back side, and fold from "c" to "d"

c

d

a   b

8

unfold

b

a

7

unfold from "a" to "b"

fold from "a" to "b" on the back side

5

a   b

fold from "a" to "b"

a

b

6

38

🔲 tomono ta

Airplane 13

I sheet in A4 or letter size format

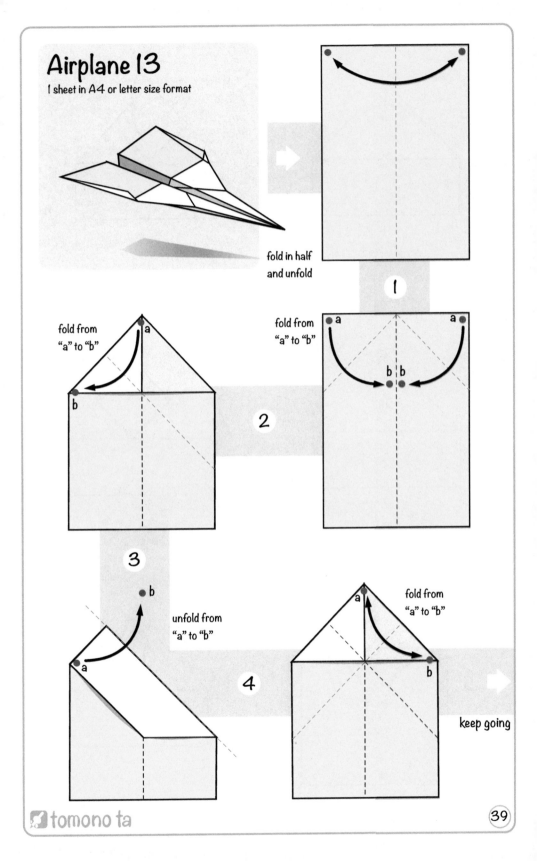

fold in half and unfold

1

fold from "a" to "b"

2

fold from "a" to "b"

3

unfold from "a" to "b"

4

fold from "a" to "b"

keep going

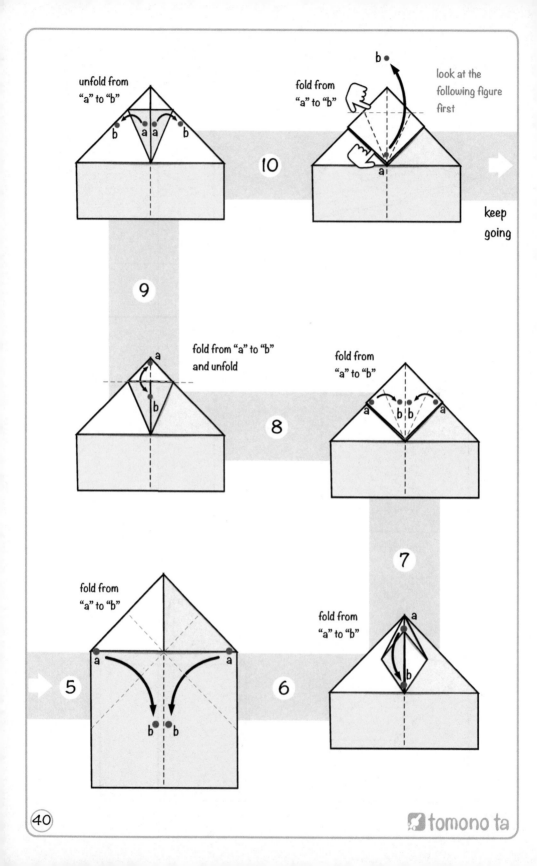

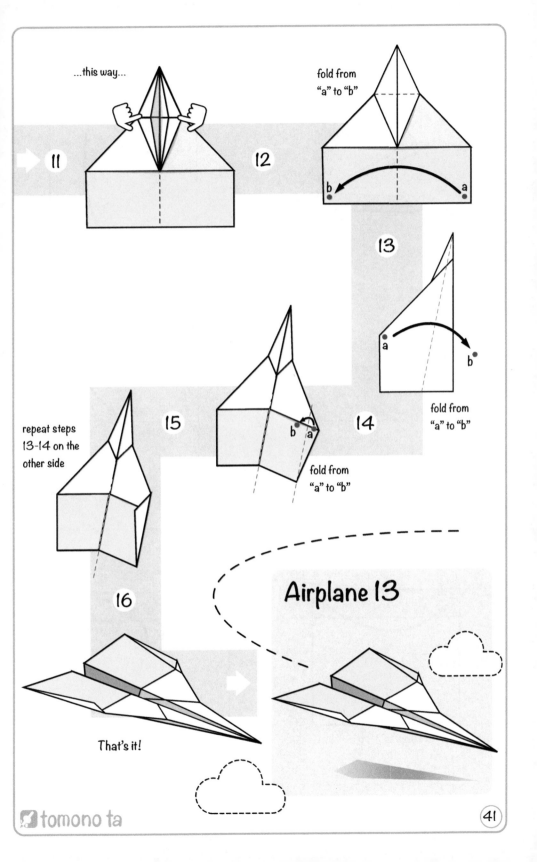

...this way...

11

12 fold from "a" to "b"

b   a

13

14 fold from "a" to "b"

a   b

15 fold from "a" to "b"

b a

repeat steps 13-14 on the other side

16

That's it!

Airplane 13

Airplane 14

1 sheet in A4 or letter size format

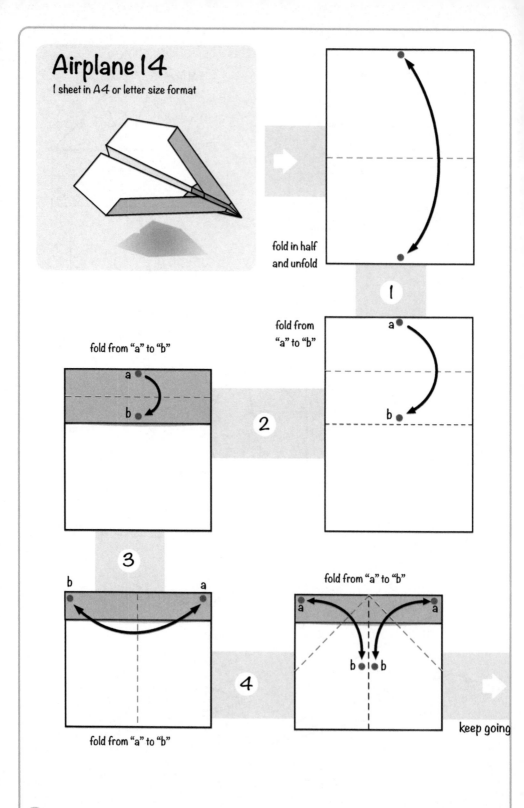

fold in half
and unfold

1

fold from
"a" to "b"

2

fold from "a" to "b"

3

fold from "a" to "b"

4

fold from "a" to "b"

fold from "a" to "b"

keep going

tomono ta

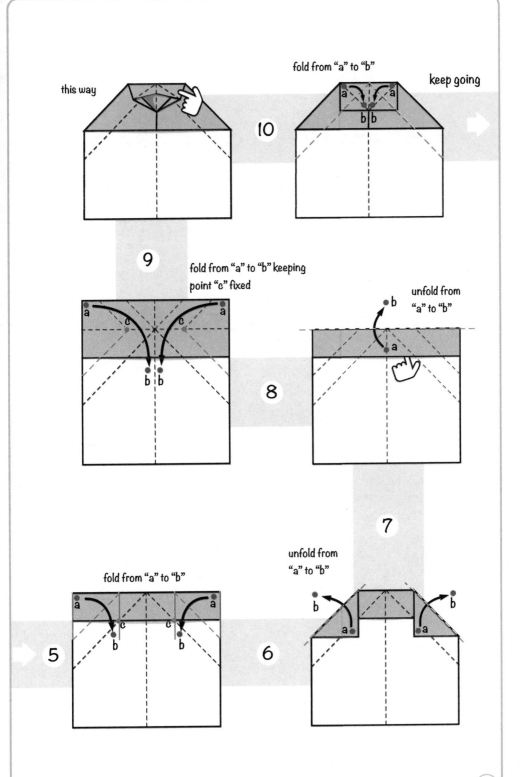

this way

fold from "a" to "b"

keep going

10

9

fold from "a" to "b" keeping
point "c" fixed

unfold from
"a" to "b"

8

7

unfold from
"a" to "b"

fold from "a" to "b"

5

6

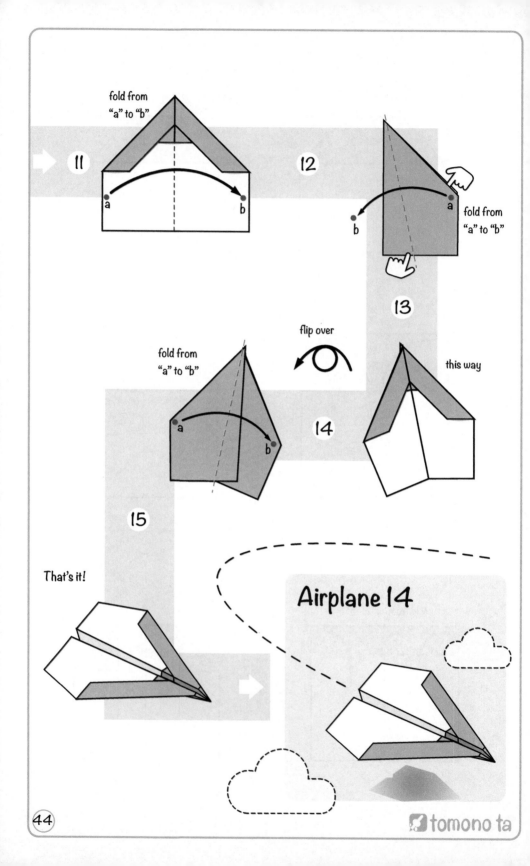

fold from "a" to "b"

11

a

b

12

fold from "a" to "b"

a

b

13

flip over

fold from "a" to "b"

a

b

14

this way

15

That's it!

Airplane 14

tomono ta

Airplane 15

1 sheet in A4 or letter size format

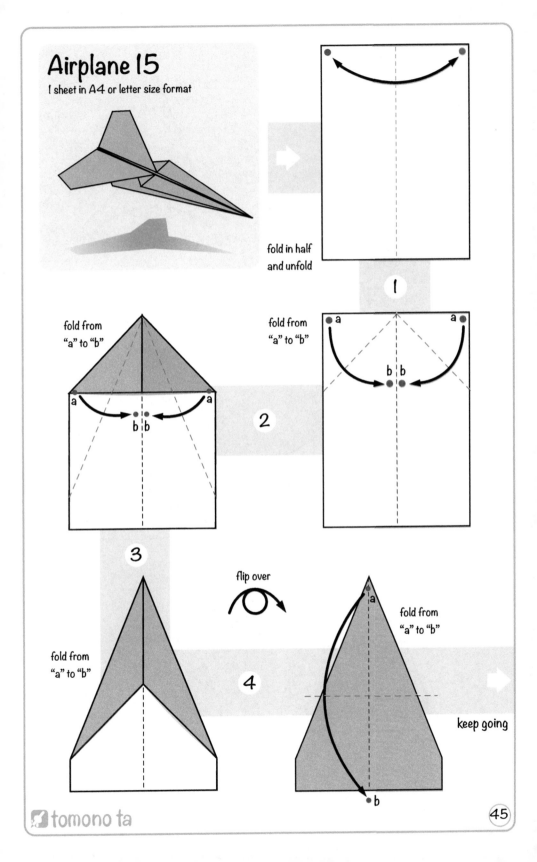

fold in half and unfold

1

fold from "a" to "b"

2

fold from "a" to "b"

3

fold from "a" to "b"

flip over

4

fold from "a" to "b"

keep going

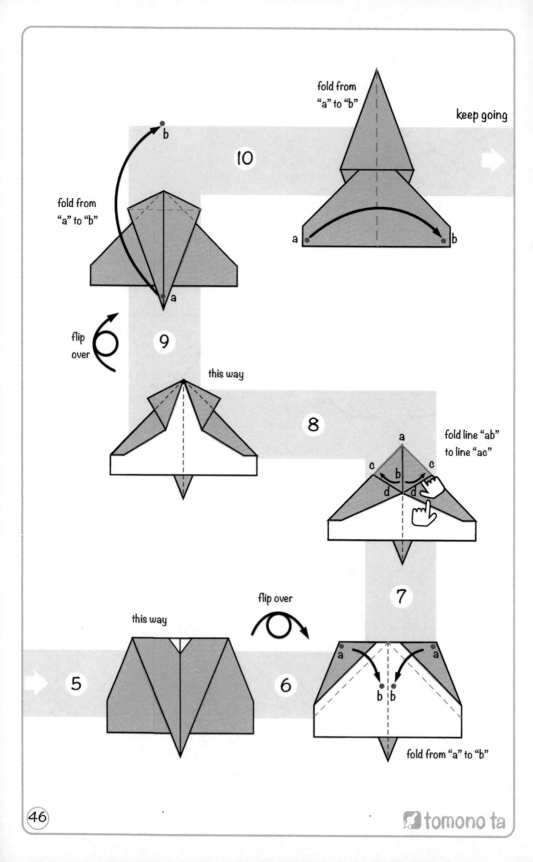

fold from "a" to "b"

keep going

10

fold from "a" to "b"

b

a

a   b

flip over

9

this way

8

a

c   b   c

d   d

fold line "ab" to line "ac"

this way

flip over

7

6

a   a

b b

fold from "a" to "b"

5

tomono ta

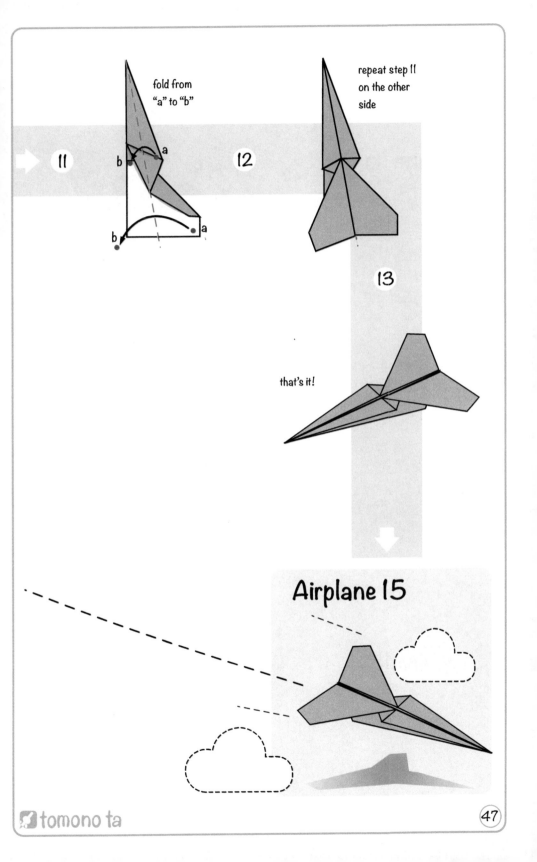

fold from
"a" to "b"

11

b
a
b
a

12

repeat step 11
on the other
side

13

that's it!

Airplane 15

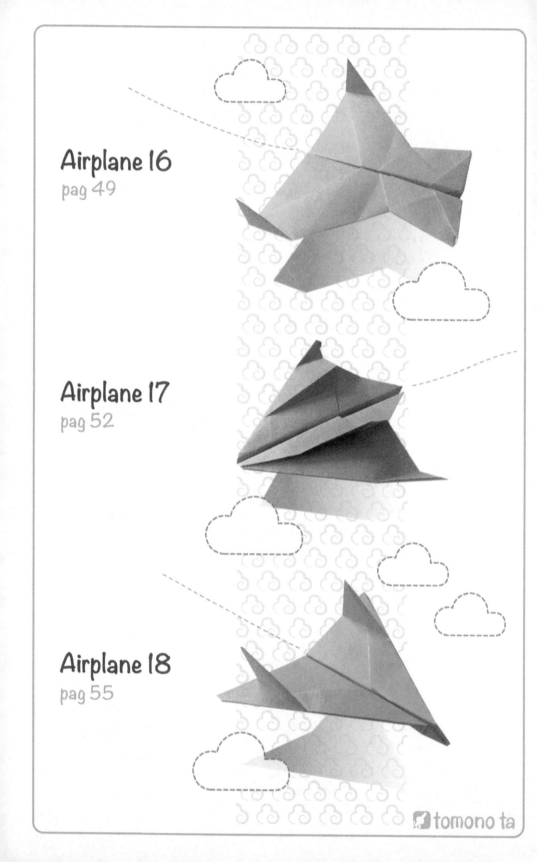

Airplane 16

Airplane 17

Airplane 18

tomono ta

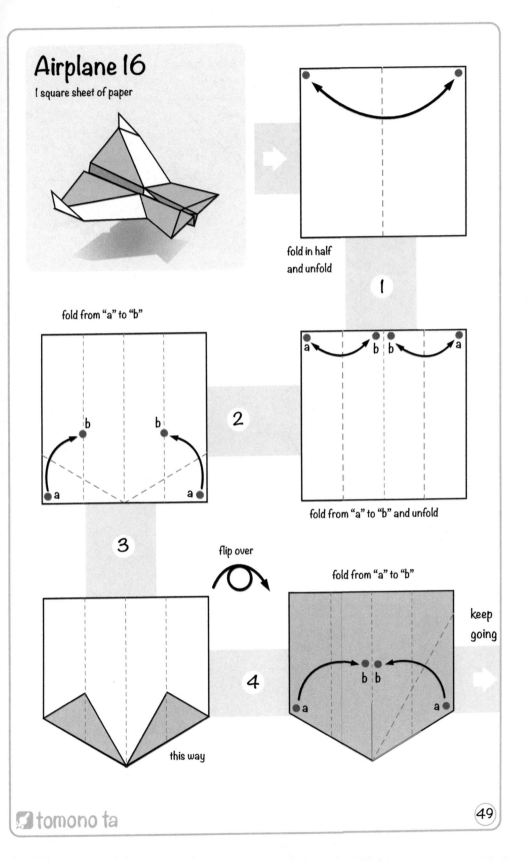

Airplane 16

1 square sheet of paper

fold in half
and unfold

1

fold from "a" to "b" and unfold

2

fold from "a" to "b"

3

this way

flip over

fold from "a" to "b"

4

keep
going

tomono ta

49

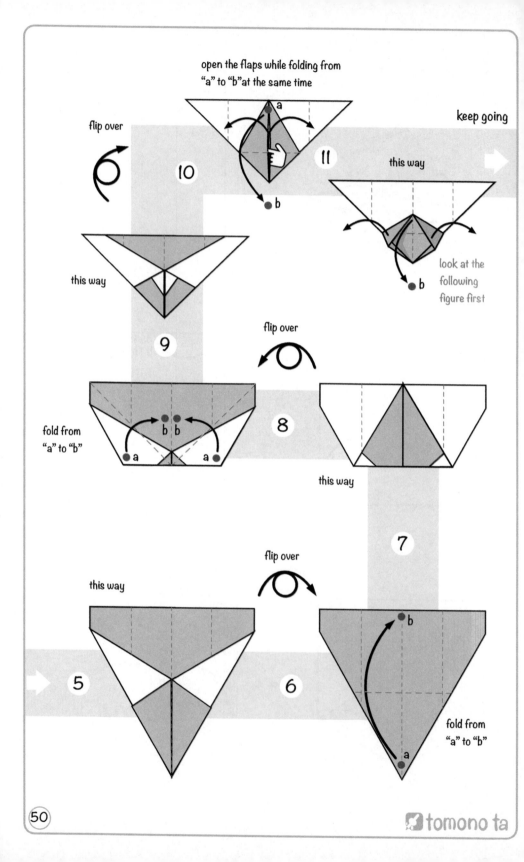

open the flaps while folding from "a" to "b" at the same time

keep going

flip over

this way

look at the following figure first

flip over

fold from "a" to "b"

this way

flip over

this way

fold from "a" to "b"

tomono ta

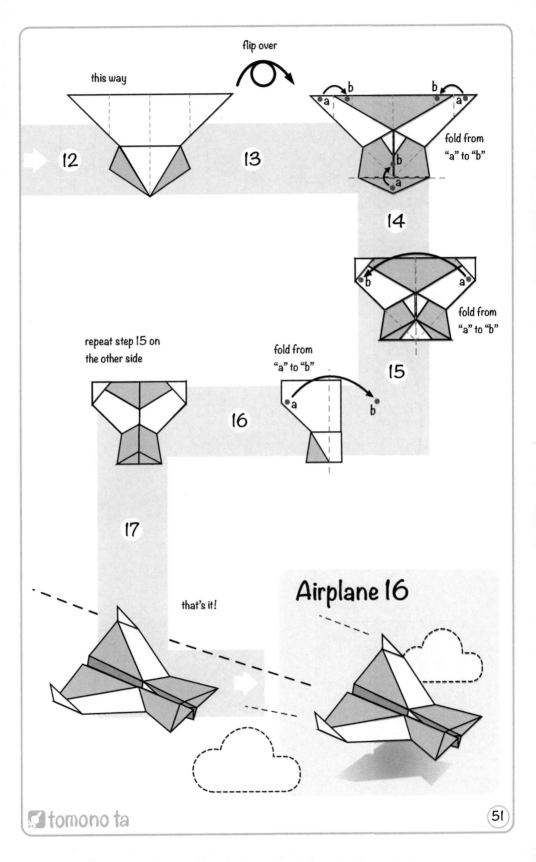

flip over

this way

12

13

fold from "a" to "b"

14

fold from "a" to "b"

15

repeat step 15 on the other side

fold from "a" to "b"

16

17

that's it!

Airplane 16

tomono ta

51

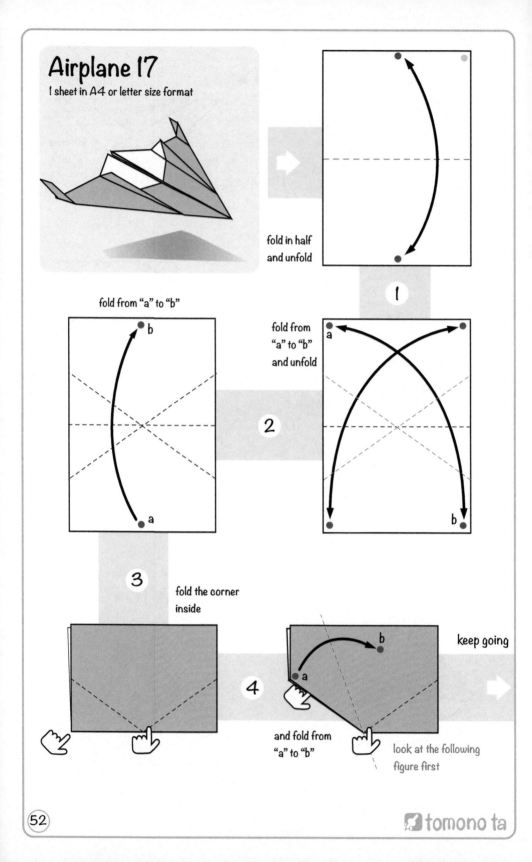

Airplane 17
1 sheet in A4 or letter size format

fold in half and unfold

1

fold from "a" to "b" and unfold

2

fold from "a" to "b"

3

fold the corner inside

4

and fold from "a" to "b"

keep going

look at the following figure first

52

tomono ta

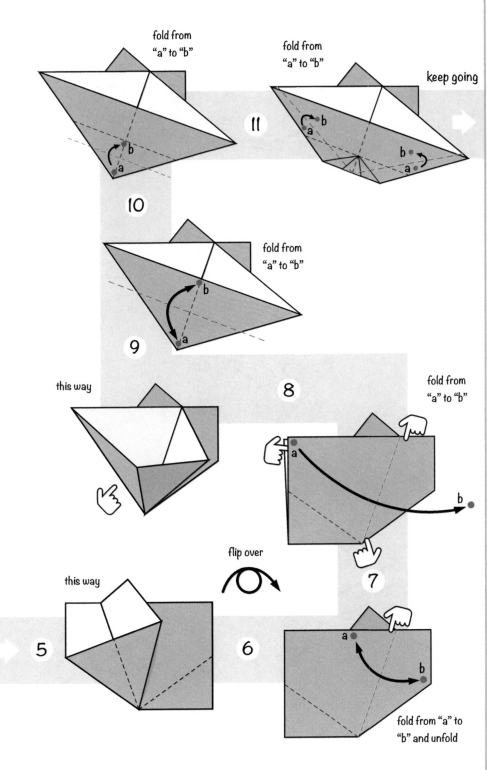

fold from "a" to "b"

fold from "a" to "b"

keep going

11

10

a
b

b
a

b
a

fold from "a" to "b"

9

b
a

this way

8

fold from "a" to "b"

a

b

flip over

this way

5

6

a

b

fold from "a" to "b" and unfold

7

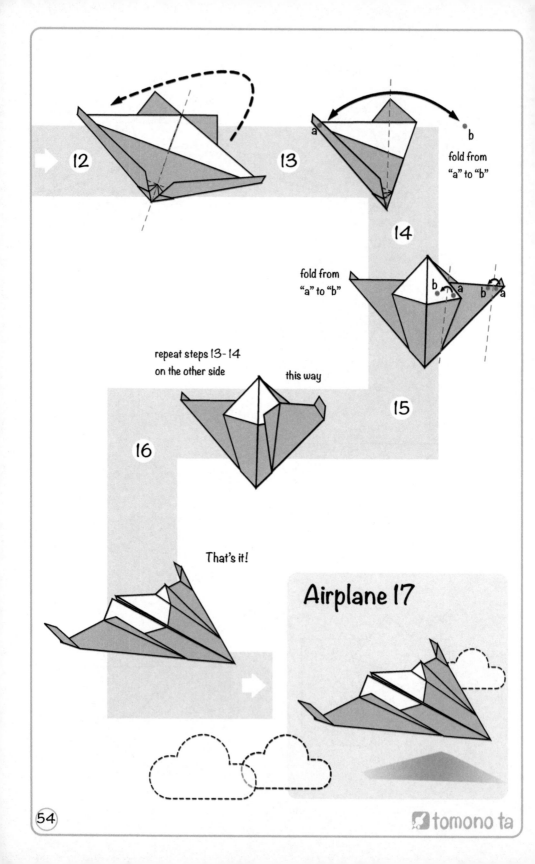

12

13

14
fold from
"a" to "b"

a   b

15
fold from
"a" to "b"

b a   b a

repeat steps 13-14
on the other side

this way

16

That's it!

Airplane 17

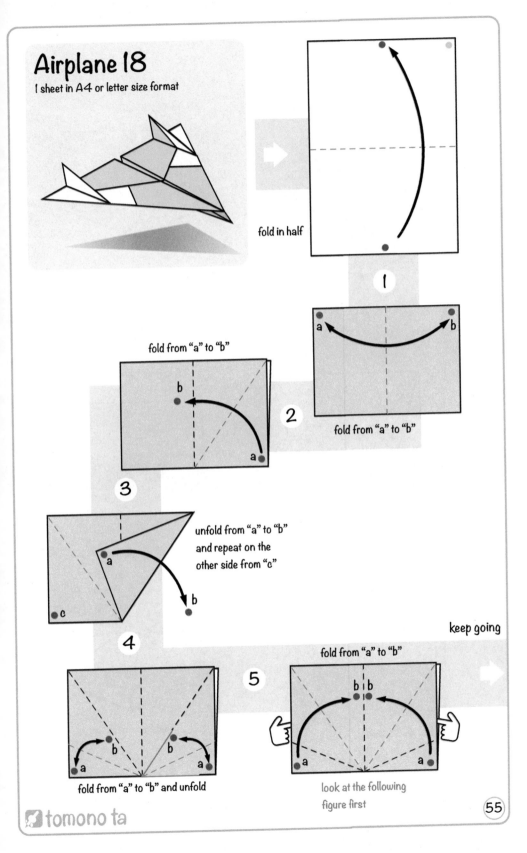

Airplane 18

I sheet in A4 or letter size format

fold in half

1

fold from "a" to "b"

2

fold from "a" to "b"

fold from "a" to "b"

3

unfold from "a" to "b"
and repeat on the
other side from "c"

4

keep going

fold from "a" to "b"

5

fold from "a" to "b" and unfold

look at the following
figure first

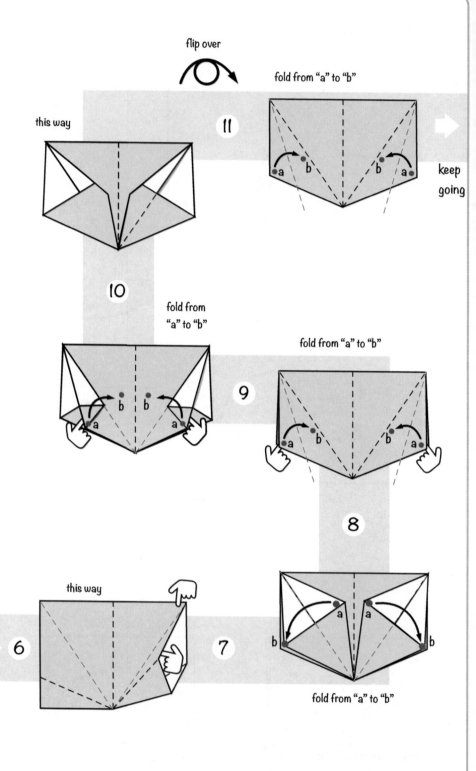

flip over

fold from "a" to "b"

this way

11

keep going

10

fold from "a" to "b"

9

fold from "a" to "b"

8

this way

6

7

fold from "a" to "b"

56

tomono ta

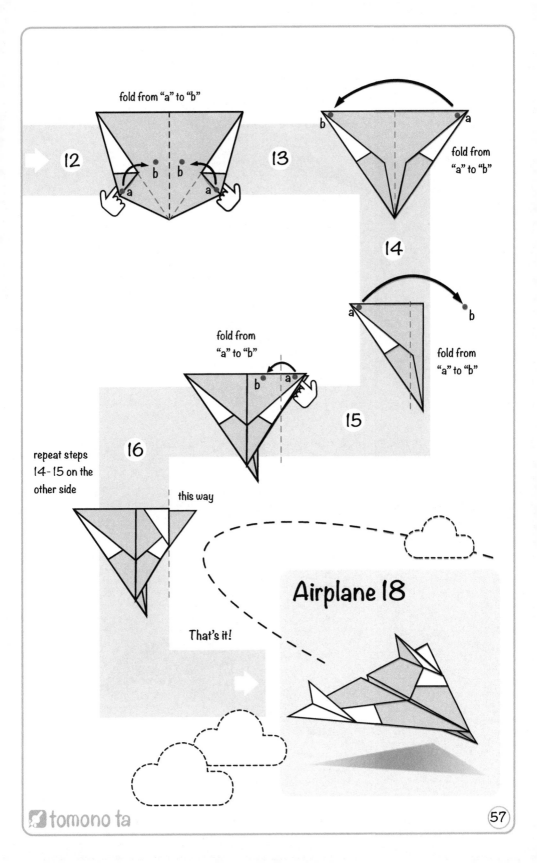

fold from "a" to "b"

12

13 fold from "a" to "b"

14

fold from "a" to "b"

15 fold from "a" to "b"

16 fold from "a" to "b"

repeat steps 14-15 on the other side

this way

That's it!

Airplane 18

tomono ta

57

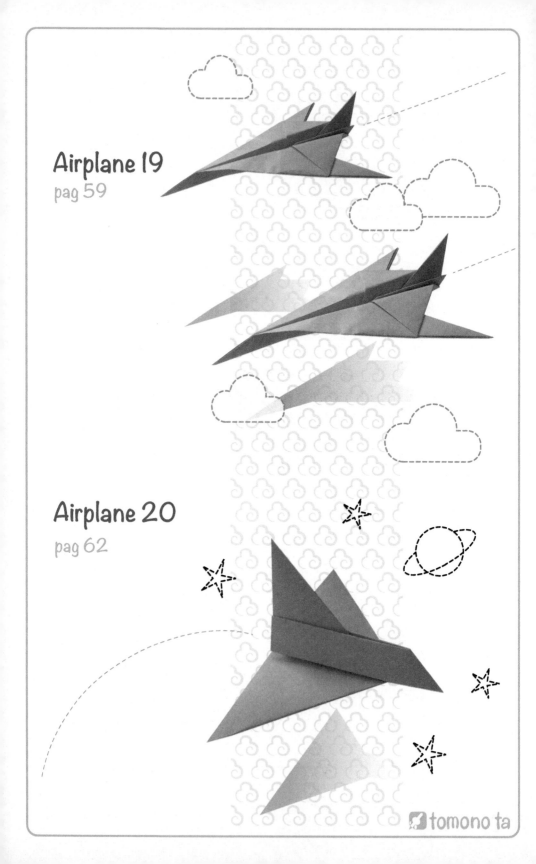

Airplane 19
pag 59

Airplane 20
pag 62

tomono ta

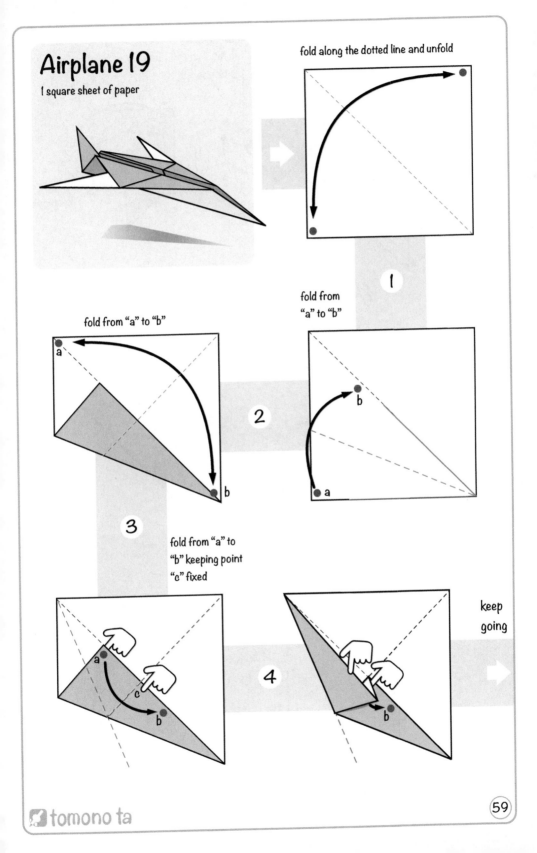

Airplane 19

1 square sheet of paper

fold along the dotted line and unfold

1

fold from "a" to "b"

2

fold from "a" to "b"

3

fold from "a" to "b"

fold from "a" to "b" keeping point "c" fixed

4

keep going

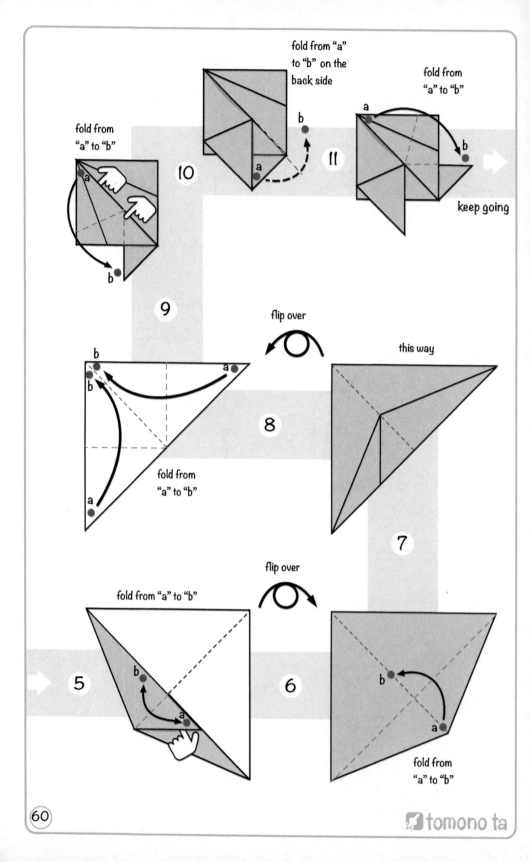

tomono ta

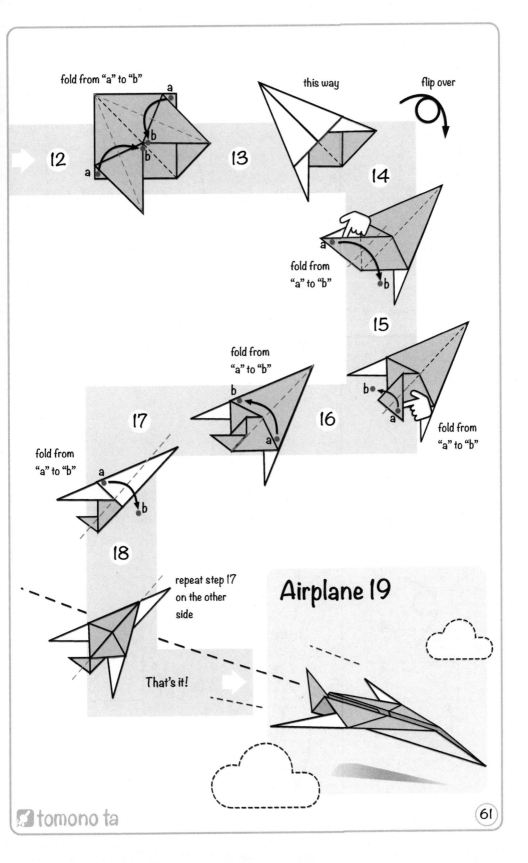

fold from "a" to "b"

12

13 this way

flip over

14

15 fold from "a" to "b"

16 fold from "a" to "b"

fold from "a" to "b"

17 fold from "a" to "b"

18 fold from "a" to "b"

repeat step 17 on the other side

That's it!

Airplane 19

tomono ta

Airplane 20

I square sheet of paper

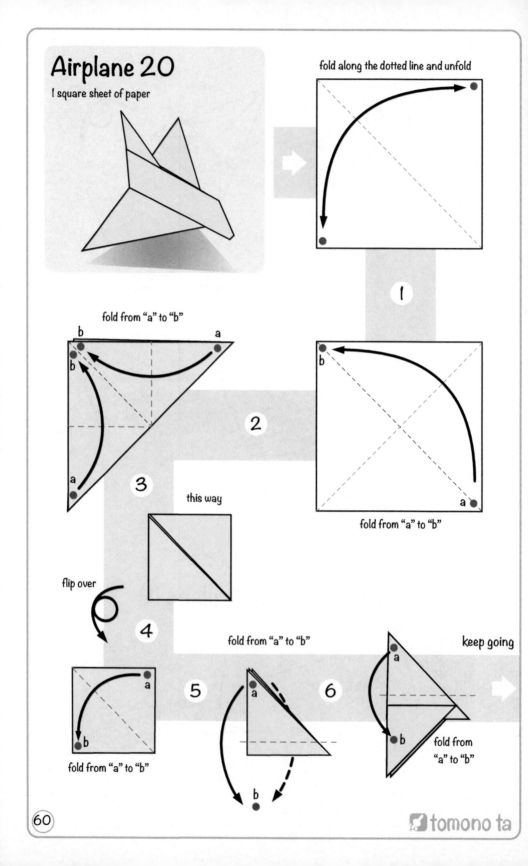

fold along the dotted line and unfold

1

fold from "a" to "b"

2

fold from "a" to "b"

fold from "a" to "b"

b   b   a

3

this way

flip over

4

5   fold from "a" to "b"

6   fold from "a" to "b"

keep going

fold from "a" to "b"

tomono ta

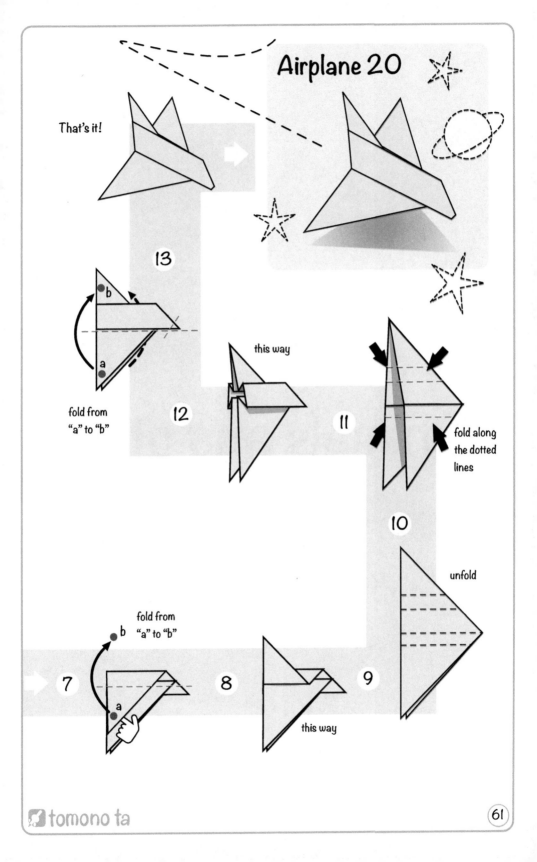

Airplane 20

That's it!

13

b

a

fold from
"a" to "b"

12

this way

11

fold along
the dotted
lines

10

unfold

fold from
b   "a" to "b"

7   a   8   9

this way

Animals and others

Animals

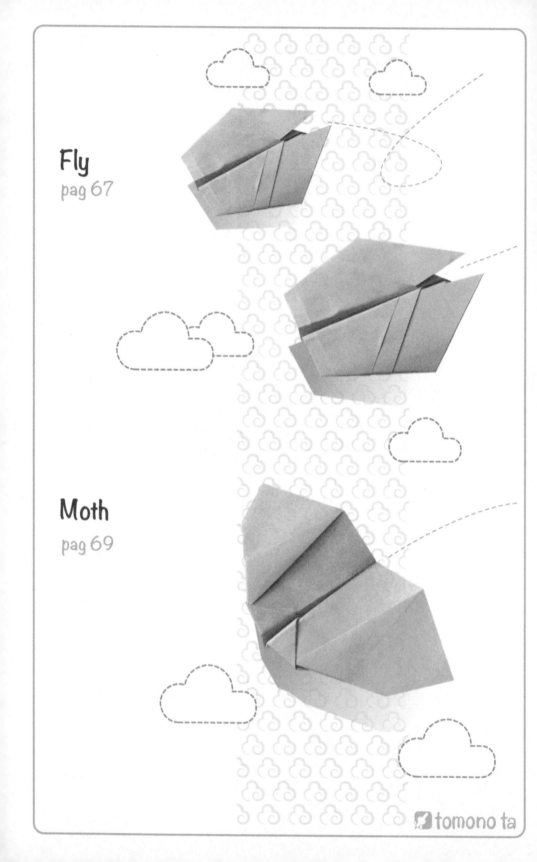

Fly
pag 67

Moth
pag 69

tomono ta

Fly

1 square sheet of paper

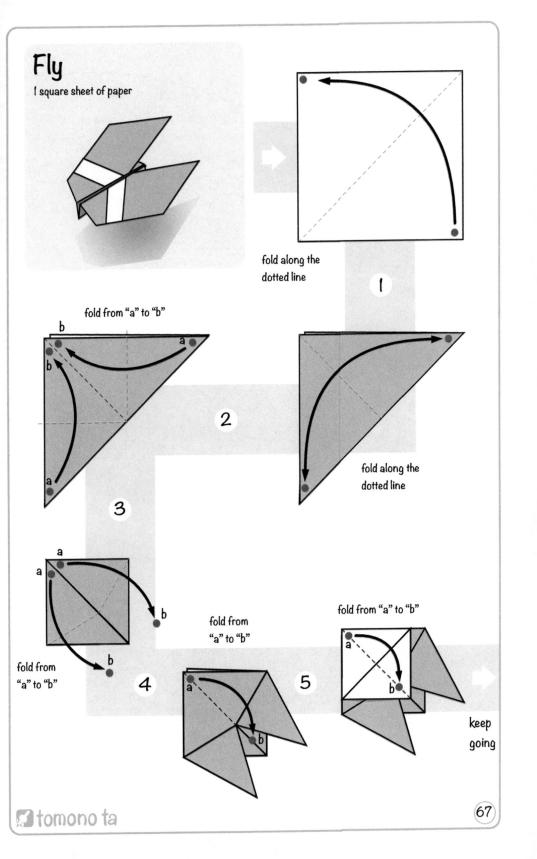

fold along the
dotted line

1

fold from "a" to "b"

2

fold along the
dotted line

3

fold from
"a" to "b"

4

fold from
"a" to "b"

5

fold from "a" to "b"

keep
going

Fly

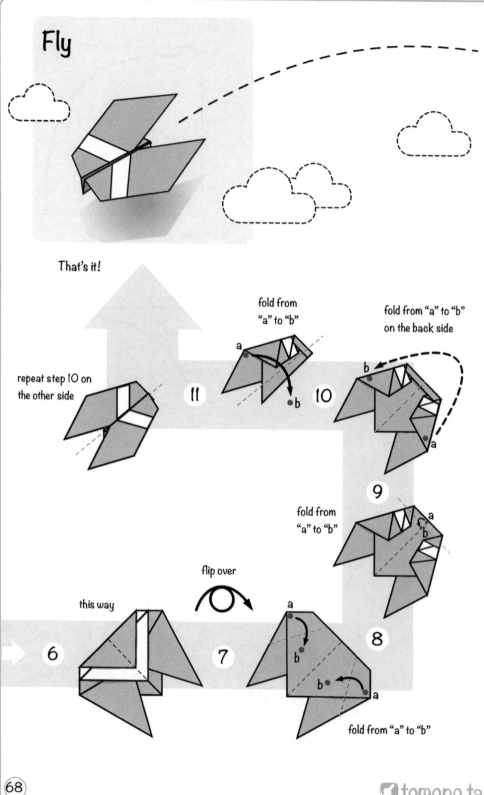

That's it!

repeat step 10 on the other side

11

fold from "a" to "b"

a

b

10

fold from "a" to "b" on the back side

b

a

9

fold from "a" to "b"

a
b

8

flip over

this way

6

7

a

b

b

a

fold from "a" to "b"

tomono ta

Moth

1 sheet in A4 or letter size format

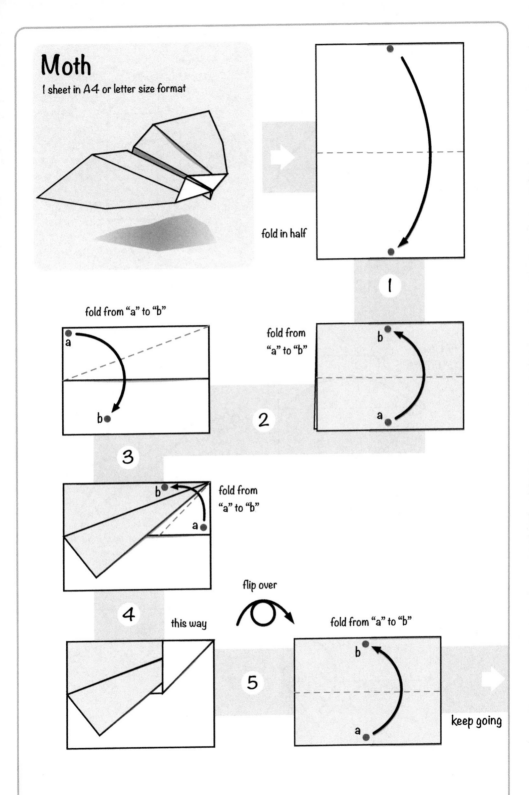

fold in half

1

fold from "a" to "b"

fold from "a" to "b"

2

3

fold from "a" to "b"

4

this way

flip over

5

fold from "a" to "b"

keep going

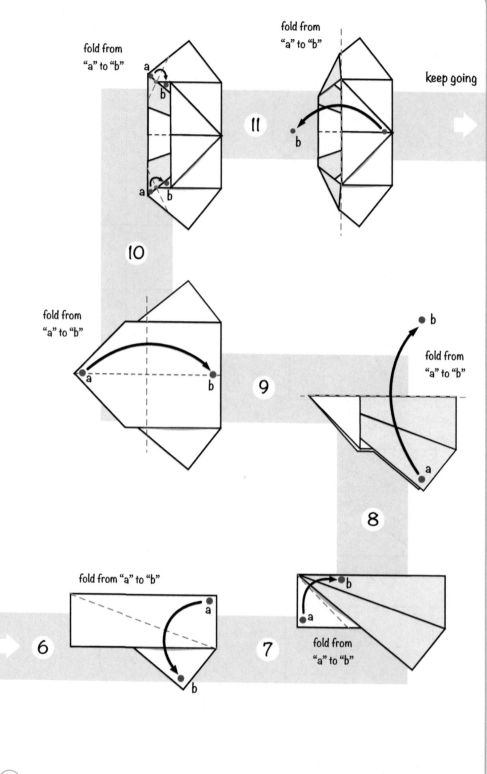

tomono ta

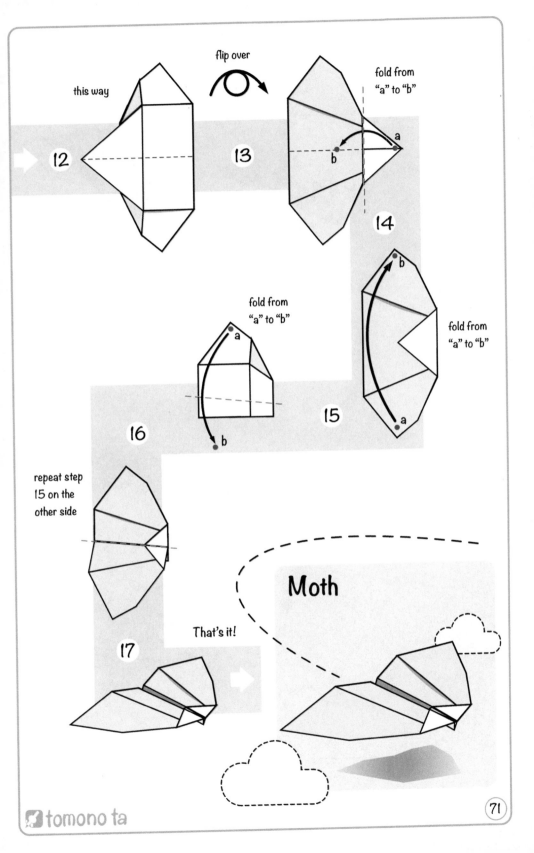

this way

flip over

12

13

fold from "a" to "b"

a

b

14

fold from "a" to "b"

b

fold from "a" to "b"

a

15

fold from "a" to "b"

a

b

16

repeat step 15 on the other side

That's it!

17

Moth

Bat
pag 73

Bird
pag 74

tomono ta

Bat

1 sheet in A4 or letter size format

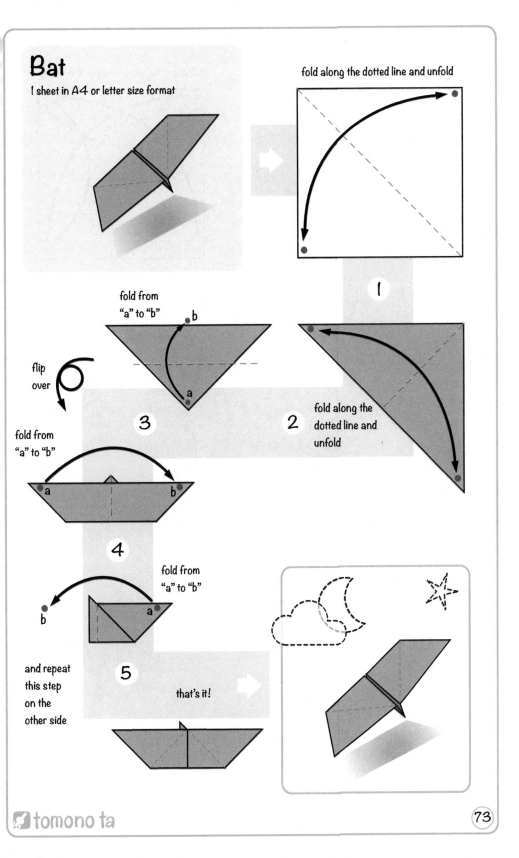

fold along the dotted line and unfold

1

fold along the dotted line and unfold

2

fold from "a" to "b"

flip over

3

fold from "a" to "b"

4

fold from "a" to "b"

5

and repeat this step on the other side

that's it!

Swallow

1 sheet in A4 or letter size format

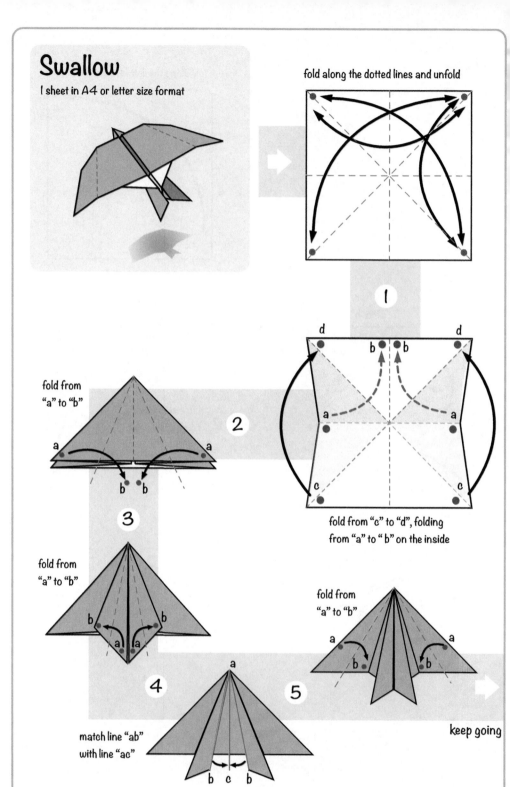

fold along the dotted lines and unfold

1

2

fold from "c" to "d", folding from "a" to "b" on the inside

fold from "a" to "b"

3

fold from "a" to "b"

4

match line "ab" with line "ac"

5

fold from "a" to "b"

keep going

tomono ta

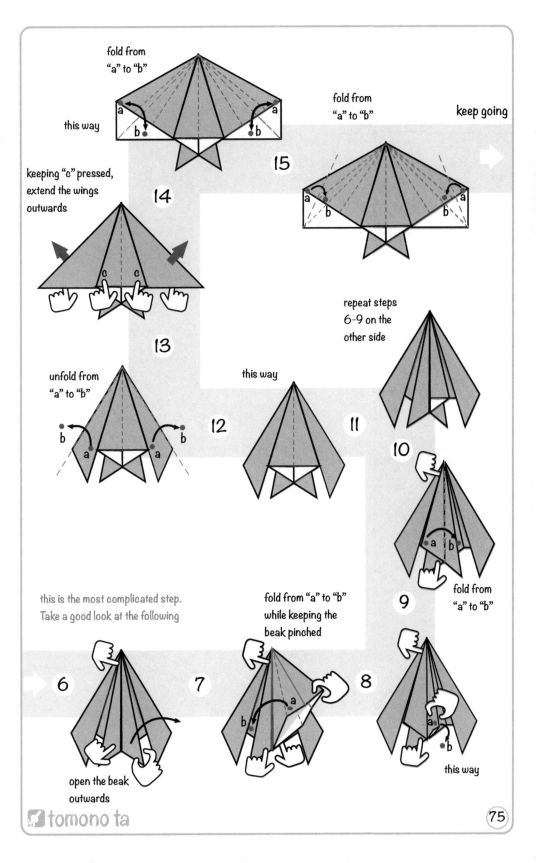

fold from "a" to "b"

this way

keeping "c" pressed, extend the wings outwards

14

13

unfold from "a" to "b"

12

this way

11

fold from "a" to "b"

15

keep going

repeat steps 6-9 on the other side

10

9

fold from "a" to "b"

this is the most complicated step. Take a good look at the following

6

open the beak outwards

7

fold from "a" to "b" while keeping the beak pinched

8

this way

tomono ta

75

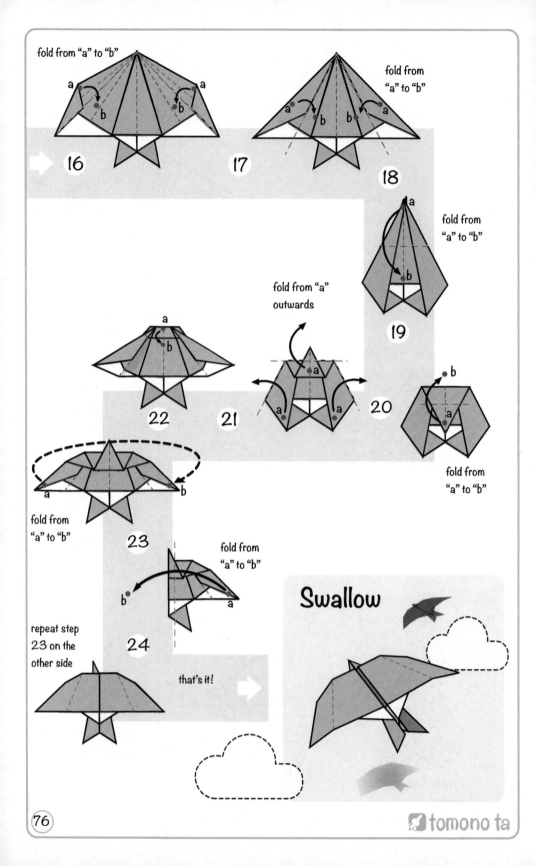

fold from "a" to "b"

16

17 fold from "a" to "b"

18

19 fold from "a" to "b"

fold from "a" outwards

20

21

22

23 fold from "a" to "b"

b

fold from "a" to "b"

24 fold from "a" to "b"

repeat step 23 on the other side

that's it!

Swallow

tomono ta

Others

Rocket

Ninja Star

Rocket

I sheet in A4 or letter size format

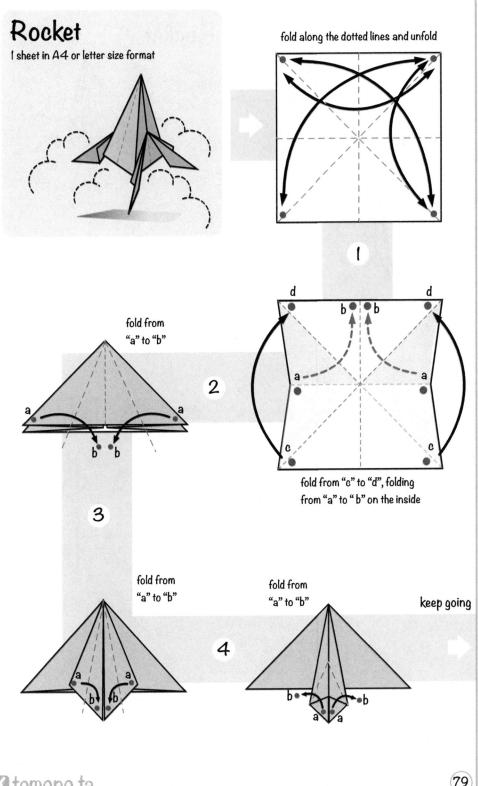

fold along the dotted lines and unfold

1

2

fold from "a" to "b"

fold from "c" to "d", folding from "a" to "b" on the inside

3

4

fold from "a" to "b"

fold from "a" to "b"

keep going

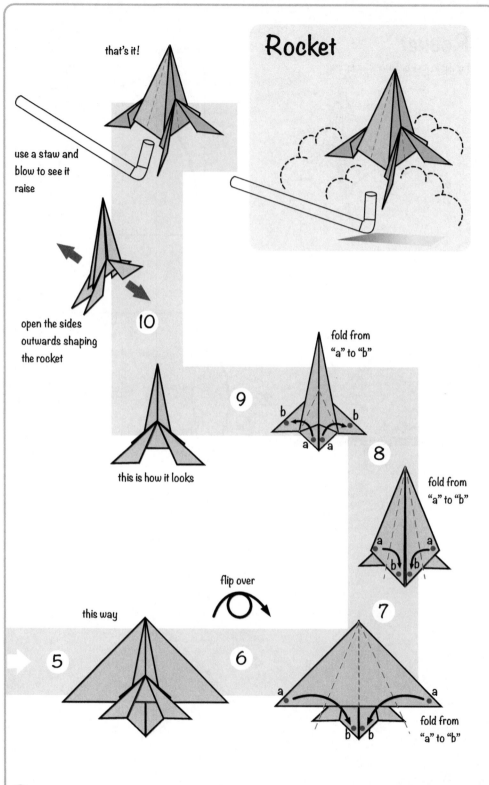

that's it!

Rocket

use a staw and blow to see it raise

open the sides outwards shaping the rocket

10

this is how it looks

9

fold from "a" to "b"

b   b
  a a

8

fold from "a" to "b"

a   a
  b b

7

flip over

this way

5

6

a   a

b b

fold from "a" to "b"

80

tomono ta

Ninja Star

I sheet in A4 or letter size format

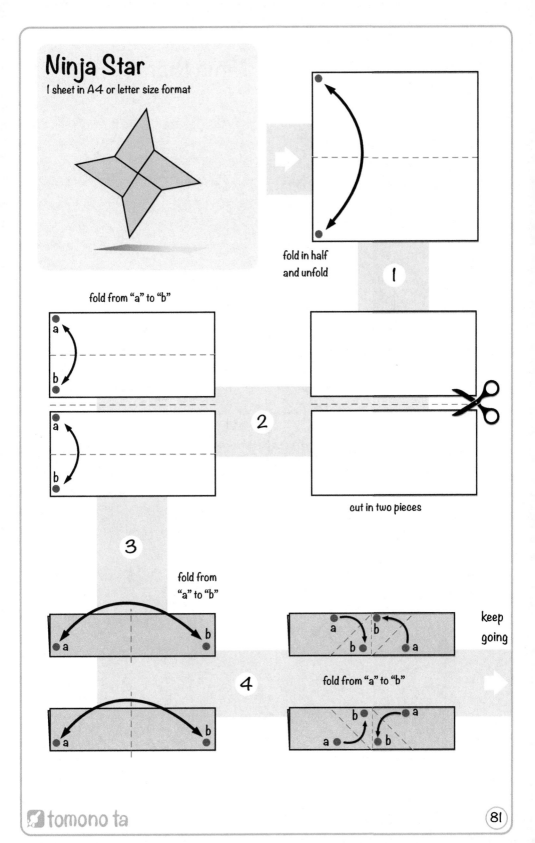

fold in half and unfold

1

fold from "a" to "b"

2

cut in two pieces

3

fold from "a" to "b"

4

fold from "a" to "b"

keep going

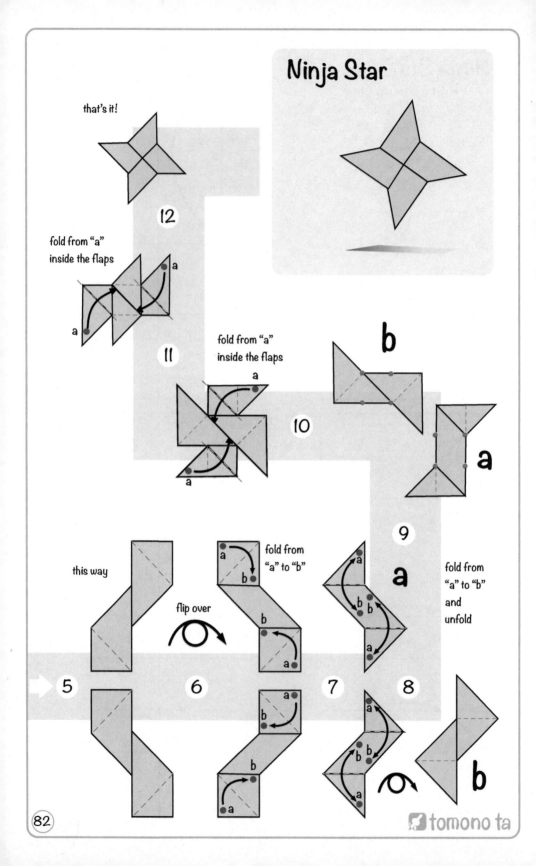

Ninja Star

that's it!

12

fold from "a"
inside the flaps

11

fold from "a"
inside the flaps

10

b

a

9

a

fold from
"a" to "b"

this way

flip over

fold from
"a" to "b"
and
unfold

5   6   7   8

b

tomono ta

Your reviews

Airplane 01

pag 11

rating:

- design   ☆ ☆ ☆ ☆ ☆
- flight   ☆ ☆ ☆ ☆ ☆
- difficulty   ☆ ☆ ☆ ☆ ☆
- general   ☆ ☆ ☆ ☆ ☆

- more:

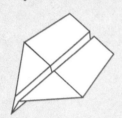

Airplane 02

pag 13

rating:

- design   ☆ ☆ ☆ ☆ ☆
- flight   ☆ ☆ ☆ ☆ ☆
- difficulty   ☆ ☆ ☆ ☆ ☆
- general   ☆ ☆ ☆ ☆ ☆

- more:

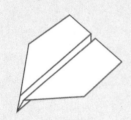

Airplane 03

pag 15

rating:

- design   ☆ ☆ ☆ ☆ ☆
- flight   ☆ ☆ ☆ ☆ ☆
- difficulty   ☆ ☆ ☆ ☆ ☆
- general   ☆ ☆ ☆ ☆ ☆

- more:

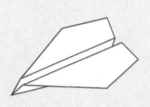

Airplane 04

pag 19

rating:

- design   ☆ ☆ ☆ ☆ ☆
- flight   ☆ ☆ ☆ ☆ ☆
- difficulty   ☆ ☆ ☆ ☆ ☆
- general   ☆ ☆ ☆ ☆ ☆

- more:

tomono ta

Airplane 05

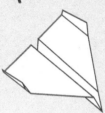

pag 21

rating:

- design ☆☆☆☆☆
- flight ☆☆☆☆☆
- difficulty ☆☆☆☆☆
- general ☆☆☆☆☆

- more:

Airplane 06

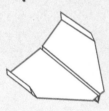

pag 23

rating:

- design ☆☆☆☆☆
- flight ☆☆☆☆☆
- difficulty ☆☆☆☆☆
- general ☆☆☆☆☆

- more:

Airplane 07

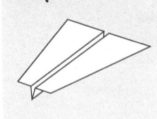

pag 25

rating:

- design ☆☆☆☆☆
- flight ☆☆☆☆☆
- difficulty ☆☆☆☆☆
- general ☆☆☆☆☆

- more:

Airplane 08

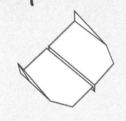

pag 27

rating:

- design ☆☆☆☆☆
- flight ☆☆☆☆☆
- difficulty ☆☆☆☆☆
- general ☆☆☆☆☆

- more:

Airplane 09

pag 29

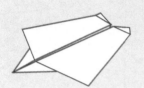

rating:

- design   ☆ ☆ ☆ ☆ ☆
- flight   ☆ ☆ ☆ ☆ ☆
- difficulty   ☆ ☆ ☆ ☆ ☆
- general   ☆ ☆ ☆ ☆ ☆

- more:

Airplane 10

pag 33

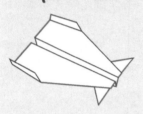

rating:

- design   ☆ ☆ ☆ ☆ ☆
- flight   ☆ ☆ ☆ ☆ ☆
- difficulty   ☆ ☆ ☆ ☆ ☆
- general   ☆ ☆ ☆ ☆ ☆

- more:

Airplane 11

pag 35

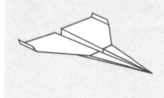

rating:

- design   ☆ ☆ ☆ ☆ ☆
- flight   ☆ ☆ ☆ ☆ ☆
- difficulty   ☆ ☆ ☆ ☆ ☆
- general   ☆ ☆ ☆ ☆ ☆

- more:

Airplane 12

pag 37

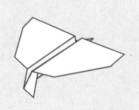

rating:

- design   ☆ ☆ ☆ ☆ ☆
- flight   ☆ ☆ ☆ ☆ ☆
- difficulty   ☆ ☆ ☆ ☆ ☆
- general   ☆ ☆ ☆ ☆ ☆

- more:

tomono ta

Airplane 13

pag 39

rating:

- design ☆☆☆☆☆
- flight ☆☆☆☆☆
- difficulty ☆☆☆☆☆
- general ☆☆☆☆☆

- more:

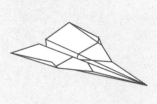

Airplane 14

pag 42

rating:

- design ☆☆☆☆☆
- flight ☆☆☆☆☆
- difficulty ☆☆☆☆☆
- general ☆☆☆☆☆

- more:

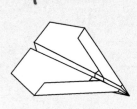

Airplane 15

pag 45

rating:

- design ☆☆☆☆☆
- flight ☆☆☆☆☆
- difficulty ☆☆☆☆☆
- general ☆☆☆☆☆

- more:

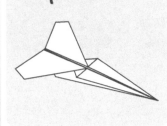

Airplane 16

pag 49

rating:

- design ☆☆☆☆☆
- flight ☆☆☆☆☆
- difficulty ☆☆☆☆☆
- general ☆☆☆☆☆

- more:

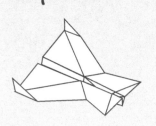

Airplane 17

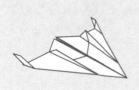

pag 52

rating:

- design ☆☆☆☆☆
- flight ☆☆☆☆☆
- difficulty ☆☆☆☆☆
- general ☆☆☆☆☆

- more:

Airplane 18

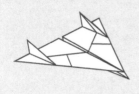

pag 55

rating:

- design ☆☆☆☆☆
- flight ☆☆☆☆☆
- difficulty ☆☆☆☆☆
- general ☆☆☆☆☆

- more:

Airplane 19

pag 59

rating:

- design ☆☆☆☆☆
- flight ☆☆☆☆☆
- difficulty ☆☆☆☆☆
- general ☆☆☆☆☆

- more:

Airplane 20

pag 62

rating:

- design ☆☆☆☆☆
- flight ☆☆☆☆☆
- difficulty ☆☆☆☆☆
- general ☆☆☆☆☆

- more:

Fly

pag 66

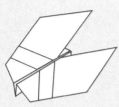

rating:

- design ☆☆☆☆☆
- flight ☆☆☆☆☆
- difficulty ☆☆☆☆☆
- general ☆☆☆☆☆

- more:

Moth

pag 68

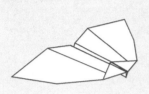

rating:

- design ☆☆☆☆☆
- flight ☆☆☆☆☆
- difficulty ☆☆☆☆☆
- general ☆☆☆☆☆

- more:

Bat

pag 72

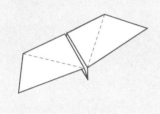

rating:

- design ☆☆☆☆☆
- flight ☆☆☆☆☆
- difficulty ☆☆☆☆☆
- general ☆☆☆☆☆

- more:

Swallow

pag 73

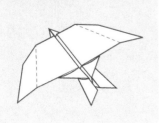

rating:

- design ☆☆☆☆☆
- flight ☆☆☆☆☆
- difficulty ☆☆☆☆☆
- general ☆☆☆☆☆

- more:

Rocket

pag 78

rating:

- design ☆ ☆ ☆ ☆ ☆
- flight ☆ ☆ ☆ ☆ ☆
- difficulty ☆ ☆ ☆ ☆ ☆
- general ☆ ☆ ☆ ☆ ☆

- more:

Ninja Star

pag 80

rating:

- design ☆ ☆ ☆ ☆ ☆
- flight ☆ ☆ ☆ ☆ ☆
- difficulty ☆ ☆ ☆ ☆ ☆
- general ☆ ☆ ☆ ☆ ☆

- more:

tomono ta

thank you!

We hope this book has been to your liking, and a big thank you for being part of this paper journey.

Printed in Great Britain
by Amazon

39957492R00056